M000285064

Candle Making Business 2021

How to Start, Grow and Run Your Own Profitable Home Based Candle Making Startup Step-by-Step in as Little as 30 days with the Most Up-to-Date Information

Clement Harrison

Your Free Gift

Want to finally turn your passion into profit and gain access to a roadmap on how to build your online store successfully?

Whether you decide to monetize your passion on the side or build a real business from what you love, you'll inevitably need an online presence.

I'd like to give you a gift as my way of saying thanks for purchasing this book. It's my 20-page PDF Action guide titled *The Online Store Game Plan: 8 Simple Steps to Create Your Profitable Online Business*

It's short enough to read quickly, but meaty enough to know the actionable steps to take when starting your online business

In *The Online Store Game Plan* you'll discover:

- How to create your online store in 8 simple steps

- 3 key pillars that will lay the foundations of your online success

- The perfect online business model for your company

- What online platform will suit your business

- Several ways to attract customers to your online store

And much more....

Scan the QR-Code Now to access *The Online Store Game Plan* and set yourself up for online success!

© Copyright 2020 - All rights reserved.

The content contained within this book may not be

reproduced, duplicated or transmitted without direct written permission from the author or the publisher.

Under no circumstances will any blame or legal responsibility be held against the publisher, or author, for any damages, reparation, or monetary loss due to the information contained within this book, either directly or indirectly.

Legal Notice:

This book is copyright protected. It is only for personal use. You cannot amend, distribute, sell, use, quote or paraphrase any part, or the content within this book, without the consent of the author or publisher.

Disclaimer Notice:

Please note the information contained within this document is for educational and entertainment purposes only. All effort has been executed to present accurate, up to date, reliable, complete information. No warranties of any kind are declared or implied. Readers acknowledge that the author is not engaged in the rendering of legal, financial, medical or professional advice. The content within this book has been derived from various sources. Please consult a licensed professional before attempting any techniques outlined in this book.

By reading this document, the reader agrees that under no circumstances is the author responsible for any losses, direct or indirect, that are incurred as a result of the use of the information contained within this document, including, but not limited to, errors, omissions, or inaccuracies.

Table of Contents

Introduction

"A beautiful room is complete with a beautiful candle."
-unknown

Candles are one of the most underrated, overlooked, and possibly misunderstood ornaments in existence. They mostly sit on shelves or somewhere in the corner of the room, and are rarely used. However, no one can deny that when the special occasion arrives, there is nothing that can match the quality and atmosphere candles offer.

Candles are seen as a symbol of romance, love, exclusivity, and everything that may come to mind. There were times when they were used only as light sources, but as electricity replaced them, they found yet another purpose to stick around. This time they were more luxurious items, used only to improve the surrounding environment and help couples, friends, and exclusive hotels to create specialized auras and aromas.

Then, there is the fact that people are now growing more conscious about being environment-friendly. They are choosing organic products over their counterparts, and that is completely acceptable. It wouldn't be wrong to say that such people are considered a niche market. Now, imagine if you could take up your hobby and convert it into a full-fledged business. You could potentially dominate this niche market which, for all intents and purposes, is still significantly large.

"But I have no idea what I need to do. I don't know if I can even do this."

If you think like that, I assure you, you aren't the only one. For starters, I too doubted if I could do this. A few years later, here I am telling you that you can certainly do it.

Everyone dreams of owning a successful business. Having one would certainly allow a lot of good things to come our way. To start with, there are the sheer profits that we can benefit from. Then, there is the fact that we own our very own business, and that is always a major morale booster. Besides, it always feels nice to do something we love, because every challenge that may come our way could be dealt with using passion, joy, and confidence.

Candle making is more than just a hobby; it is an art. I have always been fascinated with the idea of being able to create my own candles, giving them the textures I always wanted, and giving them the scents and the aromas that I loved. Initially it started as a hobby, but as time went by, my hobby turned into a passion, and that passion turned into a full-fledged business idea. Today, it continues to operate successfully, and I have had my fair share of success.

For those who love making organic candles, for those who are looking for a better business opportunity, and for those with a bit of both passions, let your quest for a business idea begin with candle making.

If you are someone who has a bit of experience making candles, you are certainly in a comfortable position to get started. This book will pick up on your existing skills and provide you with the information you need to convert your hobby into a business. *Candle Making Business 2021* will get you started on the right track.

Having the ability to create something entirely based on an idea is beyond fulfilling. It provides comfort and a sense of achievement, knowing that you can use just a few simple things and put them together to make something incredible and beautiful. Candle making does all that for you. Not only do you get to create unique blends of candles, but you can also go on to use them at home, gift them to friends, or even sell them to make some profits.

The world continues to focus more on solar energy, hybrid technology, and other giant breakthroughs, and it is evident that no one is looking at the massive opportunity that is hiding in plain sight. Even today, there are hardly more than a few good candle makers, and almost every one of them is earning a significant profit. This begs the question: if they can do that, why can't we?

By creating organic candles, not only are you providing your potential customers a better and more environment-friendly option, but you are also providing a fresh new take on organic candles.

Yet another fact is that these premade candles are expensive, albeit not too much. If you were to go on creating your own candles at home, they would be more cost-effective and economical. You can use that significant difference to gain leverage and price your candles accordingly to attract more sales. You still get a profit, the sales go up, and who knows, you may just be releasing a completely new range of candles a few years down the road.

It is all possible. All you need is a bit of guidance, patience, and creativity. Fortunately, you have it all; you just don't know it yet. *Candle Making Business 2021* will be your step-by-step guide in choosing the right material, creating sublime and exquisite organic candles, and learning how to make your own blends. It will also provide you with significant information and practical scenarios to ensure you are equipped with all the knowledge you need to get a jump-start on your start-up.

Remember, this book does not guarantee that you will succeed or fail, or achieve a certain amount of profits. There are far too many variables in place that can alter the course of your venture. As long as you stick to the basics and you manage your operations well, you should not have any issues in handling your business. How successful or otherwise your business goes on to be is absolutely up to you and your efforts. My job is simply to guide you through what you need to do to get started and make use of this incredible opportunity.

Who Should Read This?

Frankly, anyone with some basic knowledge of candle making can read this book and gain considerable knowledge on how to set up their business. However, this book is ideally intended for people between the ages of 30 to 60 years. This is because some aspects of the business may require you to have a small capital to begin with, and might require you to know a few practicalities of life.

Anyone can have a candle making business. Whether you are a 43-year-old man, stuck with a job that is going nowhere, or a 32-year-old woman, married and hoping to make the most of her time and passion while at home, this book is for you.

It is important that you should have some idea about how candles are made, what elements are used, and how you can acquire the desired outcome. If you are someone who has no idea about candle making, some aspects of this book will seem confusing. This is why it is recommended that you learn some basics of candle making before venturing on to set up your own business.

Finally, if you are someone who has no idea how to stand out from the competitors, or are intimidated by marketing and sales strategies, fear not. This book will provide you with enough information to point you in the right direction and get you started.

Who Am I?

It is only natural to find out who the author is, and what makes him the authority on said topic. My name is Clement Harrison. For the last few years, I have been selling homemade candles, and I am glad to say it has been a joy so far. I have amassed significant information, knowledge, tips, and tricks, all of which help me to progress further.

For over five years, my business has been going upwards, and I cannot recall when the last time was that I ever had to worry about my income. I have also helped quite a few people by providing them with all the information they need to get started. However, my approach was limited. I was unable to let other enthusiasts and aspiring minds know what they needed to do to set up their own start-up businesses and operate them with success. That is when it occurred to me: "I could write a book about all that I know, and help those who are trying to make their hobby into full-time profitable work."

There are many questions you may have. How to start? Where to start from? What kind of materials should you buy? What type of candles should you be making? All of these are legitimate questions, and they need appropriate answers if you are to go on and be successful. Through my book, I will provide you with all that information and more.

Not only will I be focusing on the business aspect, but I will take you through the candle making process as well. This will allow you to know exactly what you need to do. It will also help you in reducing costs and making the entire project a little more manageable.

I have always been the kind of person who believes in sharing knowledge instead of holding it back. This book, therefore, is exactly that: an effort to share the knowledge and help others achieve their success. With that said, let us get started learning all about the candle making business.

Chapter 1:
From Hobby to Business:
Making a Conscious Leap

Having a business is indeed an appealing idea. It is certainly something that everyone would love to do. It has a nice ring to it, knowing that you are the owner of a profitable business.

Right now, stop whatever you are doing and find yourself a quiet and comfortable place. Close your eyes and take a few deep breaths. As the peacefulness takes over, imagine owning a successful business. Visualize the profits flowing into your account, having all the money to meet all your expenses and still leave you with significant profits, which you can then use to do whatever you please. It feels good, doesn't it?

Fortunately, you can go on to do just that: become the owner of your very own business. Not just any business, either. This one involves you making use of the skills and hobbies that you are already familiar with.

As the famous phrase goes, you already "know the drill." All that is left now is to start changing your mindset, and start looking at things from a fresh new perspective. More specifically, you need to start looking at your hobby from a business point of view.

There will be many questions to answer, and you will have many queries as well. The idea is not to feel overwhelmed by the sheer number of these questions, but to prepare yourself and your mind to fully adapt to the changes and learn how to deal with things the right way.

This chapter will walk you through some of the core aspects of business that you need to know and learn, especially if you wish to convert your hobby into a solid business idea. Do not be intimidated by some changes, or the initial hard work that will go into making this business a success. Take it from a person who had no idea how to set this business up. I had to spend so much of my time researching on my own about everything that I eventually came to learn and experience. Had I received some guidance initially, I may have had an even more successful business by now. Fortunately for you, I will ensure you do not have to go through the hardships, and can only focus your energy on things which truly matter.

Leap to Success

I am going to assume that you already know some basics about making candles. This would help speed things up. Otherwise, I would have to explain how to make candles from scratch. For that, this book might not suffice.

One of the best ways to gain expertise in a field is through practice. Since you already know how to create a candle or two, it is time to start producing more candles than you normally would. Start by making the candles that you know and love. This could be a type of aromatic candle or just a regular candle. Both would do nicely. The idea right now is to get the word out that you are starting to change things, and that people will get to see more candles from you in the future.

Start by creating a list of people who you know personally. These could be your family members, your close friends, your colleagues at work, or even your neighbors. Try and get as many names on the list as possible. By populating this list, you are effectively creating a list of your first-ever potential customers.

Sounds nice, but there is a catch. As you make this list, remind yourself that you cannot expect them to pay you for your products.

When you need to enter a market, a perfect strategy is always to start with free samples. That is exactly what you will be doing here. You will be creating a large batch of your chosen candles and distributing them to the people around you. You can use these as gifts, especially if the recipient is celebrating a wedding anniversary. Your gifted candle would certainly brighten their day, and it would win you some favorable feedback in the future as well.

Once you have sent out your first batch of candles, try and follow up with these recipients and get some constructive feedback out of them. Some may go on to blindly praise your creation, and praise is not bad at all. However, only a few may have the courage to be honest. For those who do, hear them out without judging them.

This is something that a lot of people fail to do. They cannot withstand accepting constructive feedback or criticism. When they are presented with negative comments, or comments which go on to highlight the cons of the product, people immediately go into a state of denial.

"How dare he say my candle is no good? He has never made a candle himself. Otherwise, he would know how good an item my candle is."

The fact is that they do not need to know how to produce candles. Think about it: when was the last time major companies changed their designs or products as per the customer's need? Probably never. Successful businesses only hear out the comments and take in the criticism to learn from them. Once they identify the error, only then do they carry out the changes, if they truly are worth the shot. Otherwise, they continue doing what they do best.

Take the iPhone as an example. The world felt cheated when the iPhone 4s came along. There were so many hateful comments hurled at Apple, and it certainly made many feel like Apple had been finished. Over a decade later, they still continue to reign supreme. They still changed the design to their own liking. They continued to sell phones at a much higher price bracket, and yet the niche audience they targeted continued to pour through the gates and buy these phones.

I am not saying that you should stop paying attention to the negative comments. Not at all, as that would be wrong, and you might actually miss out on a potential opportunity. Hear these out, and see if there is a pattern. If it happens more than once, there is certainly something that needs fixing. If it is only a single comment, analyze it nonetheless.

If you believe you have collected enough data, you are good to proceed. If, however, you feel like you can still do better, do that first. Make another batch of candles, ones which are better than the earlier batch you created, and have those gifted as well. You can let the recipients know that they can refer their friends and family members to you if they like what they see. Even a single referral at the initial stage is a good sign. It means that your products are actually making a difference and are worthy of being in the market as a potential competitor to other brands.

Ask your family and friends for regular feedback. This will help you understand what your areas of strength are, such as quality, unique blend, texture, or the colors, and where your weakness lies. Just because you have something good does not mean you should ignore that

15

and only focus on the weaknesses. As a business person, you will need to take both into account and ensure that both are further polished and improved upon.

Keep track of which types of candles are getting more favorable reviews, and which ones are not up to par. This will further help you in filtering out different ideas, and sticking to the ones that you are good at. For now, you will need to produce more high-quality products. Once you have a team of people working for you, you can then find yourself in a position to take some calculated risks and explore newer ideas.

When gathering feedback, try and ask close-ended questions. Be more specific, and try to find out which specific part of your product stands out. To some, it may be the aroma it creates, while to others, it may be the quality of how your wick burns. Everything matters at this point, which is why you should find out the finest qualities first.

Finally, ask your friends and family members, and those who may have received a batch or two of your candles, if they would like you to make something specific. There may be some who would prefer you to create colorful candles, as opposed to the regular ones we see on the market. On the other hand, you may find fresh new ideas as well, like adding a certain texture or shape to the candles to give them a more appealing look and feel. Take these points into consideration as well. As long as you do not go on to compromise on your quality, you can experiment with some of these new tips and suggestions.

Once you have enough feedback, start reviewing it. On a separate list, note down what aspects of your products stood out. Note them down, as you will need to use these in the future. At the same time, use a section of the list to note down some areas for improvement as well.

Moving One Step Further

Now that you have your design eye in, it is time to start thinking seriously about your products. The next thing on the list will be to start producing these candles on a much larger scale. This will be quite a leap, especially considering that you will now need to use most of your available time to produce a large number of these candles every day.

This may seem a cumbersome task, but it is vital that you carry out this task on your own. The benefits of doing so will be discussed in a later chapter.

Creating candles on a larger scale will mean that you must get a hold of a reliable supplier. You will need to opt for quality material, and for that, you will need to start shopping around the market a bit. Unfortunately, there is no fixed solution to this, and this part of the business requires a person to invest their time in researching the finest alternatives available within the market.

The idea is to identify whether you are already buying the right type of material at the right price. You may be acquiring a good quality source material, but you may be charged with unfair prices. The internet helps, but it is only a doorway to limited knowledge. You will need to look around in the market to find out the best deals you can find, without compromising on the quality.

Remember, buying quality material allows you to create quality products. Consider this an investment that will eventually go on to affect your profit margins. If you are able to buy the highest quality material at a reasonable or fair price, your profit margins will go through the roof. No one, and I do mean no one, says no to quality merchandise. If you can offer your potential customers a promising quality product, there is no reason why they would say no to it.

To get a head-start on things, start looking around for:

- Chain retailers
- Wholesalers
- Online retailers
- Craft stores
- Farms
- Beekeepers

It is understandable that, at first, you may prefer going to your local hobby store to buy the supplies you need. However, you should know that as the business starts to grow, you will need to move towards a wholesaler to buy your materials in bulk quantity. It will be more economical, and it will allow you to enhance your profit margins further as well. Once again, ensure that your quality either remains the same or moves up a notch. Anything other than that would spell doom for your business.

You can always check around large stores and look on Amazon or other online platforms and retailers. You may be able to find something that catches your attention. They may be worth a try, but if you aren't too sure, you can always start by ordering a small amount of material. This would serve as an experiment, and it would allow you to make an informed decision on which channel you would prefer to use as your primary source of materials.

You can also take advantage of the vendor's new offerings. This not only allows you to source new materials at a lower price, but it is also a great way to know what the current market trend is. That can often provide you with better opportunities and ideas to pursue.

The vendor you choose must be able to offer you the quantities you may need or require in the future. If they are unable to do so, it is best to look for someone who can. You do not wish to be caught in a situation where you have pending orders, and you run short on supplies. Canceling such orders, therefore, would be the only solution, and that can hurt the business and its reputation massively.

The duration of delivery also matters. There is no point in ordering materials from a vendor who will take 15 to 20 days for delivery. You might still miss out on a lot of orders, and you may be forced to cancel a few just to save yourself from the embarrassment. Be sure to check with the vendor about the delivery time and the availability of items before you place your order.

While searching online, you may come across some popular names, such as CandleChem.com, or CandleMakingSupplies.net. Both of these are highly reputable, and are known to be excellent options for those seeking to create quality candles.

CandleChem.com offers you a wide range of products, including:

- Seamless molds
- Warning labels
- Braided wicks

CandleMakingSupplies.net provides a good range of waxes, molds, and containers. Regardless of which you choose, be sure to check the quality. Even the best of companies can at times provide you with sub-par materials.

Wholesalers - Things to Know

There is no denying that wholesalers will always provide you with the most attractive prices for the kind of material you are after. However, to fully take advantage of their prices, you will need to buy in a bulk quantity, and that can be a bit of a problem for someone who has yet to begin their business.

At this point in time, you may only be catering to a few requests, perhaps a customer or two. However, it will not always be the same. You will eventually start getting larger orders, and you may even start getting more orders than you can manage to produce. If you are able to map out your sales, use analytical and forecasting tools, offered free on Excel, to predict when such a time would come. It is best to be fully prepared for that.

When choosing your wholesaler, consider a few things. These include the profit margins you have set for yourself to achieve, the customer base that you currently have, and the customer base that you predict, using charts and data that you gather. Without these vital pieces of information, approaching a wholesaler may not be the best option.

The first thing is to work out your cost per product. This will require you to have a bit of knowledge about costs. If you are not too sure what you need to do to find out the cost of the product, there are many great examples available on the internet to teach you that within a few minutes. Once that is sorted, we can then move on to set up profit margins.

It is of great importance that you figure out the profit margin you seek. It could be 20%, it could be 50%, or it could even be higher than that. Depending on the type of competitors you may have in your locality, you will need to choose a price bracket that attracts potential customers and allows you to gain the profit margins you aim for, or at least be as close to it as possible.

Make it a rule of thumb that you will not buy a large number of supplies right away unless you have already worked out all these important details. You will also need to know how fast you can sell your products, so you have an idea when you can expect your stock to run out. This will further help you to order materials beforehand.

When choosing a wholesaler, always check out the reviews other customers have left on reliable platforms. If they are registered with the Better Business Bureau, search for their name online. They should have their ratings and reviews to check through. If they seem reliable, they most likely are.

In an ideal scenario, your choice of wholesaler would also have a customer service team that is ready to help you place orders, look into issues, or file complaints, should things go wrong.

To further satisfy yourself with the authenticity of the wholesaler, ask questions regarding the materials you are interested in buying. If they are able to answer with facts and figures, and you know them to be accurate, it shows that they know what they are doing. If you see a salesperson losing focus or unable to answer your questions, walk away. Never risk your money and time in the hands of people who have no idea what they are doing. They could very well lure you into buying all kinds of things, most of which will serve you no purpose.

Finally, know your budget. You cannot expect yourself to go into a wholesale store and buy in bulk without actually having the finances to back you up. Work out a realistic budget and abide by it. Do not overspend, and do not cut corners by compromising on quality. If something is not available, do not rush into buying something you are not sure of just because there is no other option available. You can always try out another store.

Scaling up your production operations will certainly mean upgrading your equipment as well. This is a vital step, and we will discuss it in detail in Chapter Two. For now, just know that you will need to keep some of your budget aside to start upgrading your tools and machines.

Gain Expertise

Whenever you start a business, customers will always look at you as an expert. They will expect you to answer their questions, resolve technical issues, and provide them with better alternatives and resolutions. If, at such times, you end up answering, "I am not too sure," you are setting yourself up for failure.

To truly be the king of the hill, you must think and act like the king of the hill. You will need to go into all the tiny details about the materials and products you have on offer. You should be able to know what it is that your product can do, and what it is that it can't do.

I have seen queries where people have asked how long my candles would burn. Had I not known that, I might have lost a significant number of customers. The impression they would have received had I said "I am not too sure" would have been anything but promising.

Know your product, know about the current trends, and know exactly what the customers want. A good way to get all the industry-related information would be to browse through the websites for Candle Cauldron and The National Candle Association. These two websites can provide you with all the related information that can help you understand the market better.

"Knowing is half the battle."

It is true. The more you get to know about things, the better chances you have to succeed. In our case, we are aiming to set up a candle making business. The more we learn about the trends, the demands, and any new opportunities in the field, the easier it will become for us to decide which direction we should choose to gain the most profits. Otherwise, we would just be like a sailboat lost in the middle of the deep blue sea, without direction or heading.

Apart from these websites, there are some other great platforms you can use to get in on the action and learn all that is happening straight from the customers and enthusiasts themselves. One such way is to utilize your social media profile accordingly.

You can use Facebook to browse through some helpful and informative pages and communities, all of which provide you with in-depth knowledge about current trends, fresh and new ideas about candle making, and some honest feedback for you to study regarding existing candles on the market as well.

I will not leave things to chance here, which is why I will share with you some of the most helpful pages and communities I have come across on Facebook. Below are some names of pages which I have personally used and found extremely helpful:

- Wood Wick
- Imperial Candles
- Bella Candles Com
- Jewelry Candles

Apart from these Facebook pages and communities, you can also sign up on various platforms. Some good examples for such platforms would include:

- CraftsForum.co.uk
- forums.bellaonline.com

Finally, my all-time favorite: Quora. It is a treasure chest of knowledge, especially for those who are pursuing business ideas, plus a lot more. You can quite literally ask a question directly from the experts, and you will be provided with a sufficient number of answers. You can easily filter out the good ones and gather the information you need to move further.

The internet is your friend, but it is not the only friend you have. There are many other ways, chief among which is your own experience. The more you practice and experiment, the quicker you'll learn about candle making and its related business.

Speaking of business, you will certainly need to know the kind of people, or market, you aim to attract. Why? Let's look into that a little more.

Become an Opportunist

I mentioned earlier how candles were once used as the primary source for light in the dark nights. Later, as electricity was brought into people's houses, the humble candle moved on to become more of a luxury item, and eventually into an ornament that still continues to fascinate the world. There is no second opinion about the fact that the market for candles has shrunk a little. However, it has not vanished at all. As long as we, the human beings who created them, remain, candles will continue to stay as well. This is a good thing. It means that we can have a perpetual market, one that will never fully dry out.

When it comes to targeting this niche market, I also mentioned that it is still a significantly large market. To begin with, it is hard to decide who we are trying to target. First we have luxurious hotels, which may order candles in bulk for their special tables. Then we have restaurants, hundreds and thousands of them. We have religious centers such as churches, mosques, and temples, and then we have communities. Besides all that, we have individuals, and they alone stack up to a number that goes into the millions, if not more. Certainly, the niche market is still too broad to cover. We will cover how to narrow down our niche market in Chapter 6, but for now, know that the potential market is huge. That should certainly make you feel a lot more comfortable.

With that said, however, if we do not know our product and if we do not go on to become an expert at what we do and what we offer, we will not be able to penetrate a market, regardless of its size.

While I have given you some incredible sources to look into, there is a lot more that needs to be done, and it can only be done through the power of research. I had to spend months just to find out what my competitors were doing and learn if there were any gaps that I could go on to exploit and use to my advantage. That actually broke the ice for me as a business owner.

Similarly, as you continue to create candles, know that there are others who may be creating exactly the same thing as you. If that is the case, you do not hold any competitive advantage. To gain some of that, you need to look at what your rival candle making businesses are doing, and what kind of products they are offering. You may be living in a locality where scented candles are not available, and the current businesses are too focused on making jewelry candles. If you identify the gap, utilize it and immediately gain all the competitive advantages in the world by offering a product that is entirely new, unique, and attractive. I assure you, if you can figure out the gap in the market, you are the next big success story.

Besides looking for gaps, learn what your competitors are doing well and try to find out what can be done to further improve upon that. They may have delicate designs, but they may not have the burning quality, or the right kind of wick. Perhaps you could manage to do what they couldn't. Sometimes, looking at a product through the eyes of a customer can often provide you with hints and clues.

It is needless to say that you will not be competing with all the big giants out there, at least not at this point in time. However, that does not mean that you cannot take a peek inside their business activities and learn what they do best, and how they are able to continue garnering success after success.

Take lessons from what they do. It is not about the large machinery or the immense workforce they have; it is always about the idea that they carry on with. Learn what they do, how they do it, and what makes their idea such a hit with people. Use these communities to get feedback about their products to understand further what they do best, and how you can incorporate some of that in your products. Some good companies worth researching are:

- Yankee Candle
- Hush Candle
- WoodWick

You can also check out Shopify and Etsy to get more ideas about the smaller businesses in operation. You will also be able to see what they are doing and what is working for them.

Besides these, there are some other candle-makers you can look into and gain further valuable insights from. Some of the ones I would recommend are:

- uscandleco.wordpress.com
- Natures Garden Candles
- Candle Warmers

So far, it is obvious that the more knowledge we gather, the better our chances will be to succeed in this field of business. We, as entrepreneurs, need all the knowledge we can gather to help us go on and achieve the results we desire. Following the same footprints of another successful organization might be a start, but following it all the way through is not a lasting solution. We need to know where we aim to go, and we need to learn from the mistakes or areas of improvements found in our competitors. Only then can we go on to attain a true competitive advantage, thus allowing us to penetrate the market effectively.

Begin your venture in the safest way possible, which is by creating the candles you create the best. The beauty of such an exercise is that it is not repetition. Instead, you are polishing your own skills and further improving them to get the maximum benefit out of them. By creating these candles, you can also figure out more about your niche markets, and that is also something we will discuss in future chapters.

Chapter 2:
Tools and Supplies for a Larger Scale: Leveling Up Your Workspace

In the previous chapter, we learned quite a lot. One of the things we briefly touched upon was the fact that we will eventually need to upgrade our equipment. Indeed, you cannot expect to create hundreds or thousands of candles a month on your own, using nothing more than your hands and some basic tools. That is virtually impossible since every human being, even the strongest one, has limited energy. To make our lives easier, upgrading our equipment will undoubtedly help us utilize our workspace better, and to be able to produce larger quantities of products.

In this chapter, we will be looking into all the equipment, tools, and supplies you will need to set yourself up for larger-scale production and operation. These will go on to contribute significantly towards your success in the candle-making business. The results may not pour in immediately, but you will soon be thanking yourself for getting the much-needed upgrades done on time.

Knowing Your Tools

Since we have decided to proceed with the idea that we will be setting up our very own candle-making business, and we have already started to gather some information, it is time to start taking some actions.

The first leg of the journey brings us through the all-important phase of acquiring the right kinds of tools, materials, and supplies. Of course, we cannot continue to create products from the limited supply we have, and we cannot rely on our local crafts and hobby stores to provide us with all the supplies we need. They would eventually run out, putting us and our production on hold. Fortunately, we learned about finding just the right kinds of sources to acquire our materials from. However, it is time to address the elephant in the room.

"What do I need to get started?"

The Workspace

Ideally speaking, your workspace, regardless of the size, will be well lit. You need all the light you can get to see better, as even the tiniest details and aspects matter significantly in the candle making business. You will need to have sufficient room so that you can work efficiently without causing clutter.

Your tools must always be organized. This helps in saving you time and energy. If you are the type of person who picks up a tool, uses it, and then leaves it there, you will eventually run into all kinds of problems, chief among which is not being able to find the required tool on time.

Since we will be working with wax and other major ingredients, not to forget flammable material, you will need to ensure that your workspace is well-ventilated. It must also be comfortable to work in, as there will be times where you will continue to work for hours at a single stretch. Having an uncomfortable workspace will cause you to develop back spasms, body aches, and even headaches.

Your workspace should have a sturdy workbench. Do not fall for the stylish ones because most of them will end up getting ruined, cut, burnt, or broken. Invest in buying a sturdy workbench that is able to accommodate your needs.

Besides a workbench, you will need a microwave.

"Hang on a minute. Am I learning about the things I need to cook?"

As surprising as this may sound, you actually do need a microwave, but not for the purpose you might have on your mind. You will need a microwave to be able to clean things easily, such as jugs and jars.

You will also require shelving for storing your tools and supplies. Once again, the more organized you are, the better the entire operation will be for you. If you can, buy little notes or use cutouts from waste paper and label them with the things that each of your shelves will hold. It is very easy to find yourself looking all around when trying to find something you may need. Having your shelves labeled will allow you to go past that obstacle and save time.

To store your materials, you will also need additional storage. Do not stuff your materials into the shelves. Let your shelves hold only tools and essential supplies. The rest can go into some storage room, box, chest, or a dedicated storage area.

As you start creating candles, you will obviously start staining your aprons, dresses, or workbench clothes. Besides, you will always have other washables lying around. It is a good idea to start thinking about the washing facility you will use. If you have significant room for washing, you may not need to look elsewhere. If not, you will need to start looking around for washing facilities which offer you economical prices and allow you to do your laundry in bulk quantity in as little time as possible.

Furthermore, you will also need access to power. Without having power, you will not be able to light up the area, nor operate certain tools to get the job done. You will also need power to power up the microwave, and any other electronic devices that may be in use.

If you live in an area where there are constant power cuts, you can save up some money to eventually buy a power generator, or install alternative energy solutions. However, be warned that the latter may not be able to power up all of your devices, and the cost may be extremely high.

Finally, once your candle making process is done, you will need to have a climate-controlled environment. This is something necessary because you will need to store your finished products at a specific temperature. If you store them in warmer conditions, the candles will be exposed to higher temperatures and they can easily melt well before they are sold, let alone used.

You do not need to maintain excessively low temperatures, which means a good air conditioning unit alone should do the trick. If you have some extra space, you can use that as your packing area as well.

It is always recommended that your packaging area and your workbenches are separate facilities or zones. This is to promote the safety of the candles as well as of the handler (that would be you), and to ensure smooth operation. It is easy to be caught in a mix of things, and you might end up packing something that wasn't supposed to be a part of the package.

Essentials You Should Have

Of course, I have not ruled out the possibility that you may already have quite a few things with you. However, to ensure that you do not miss out on something that may be needed, here is a complete list of items that are essential for any candle making business to have. If you have been making do with some equipment and tools, it is time to throw those away and invest in those that really matter.

1. **Double boiler or a rice cooker** - These will allow you to melt the wax in large quantities without any issues. The other alternative is to buy a wax melter, but for that you may have to invest at least $1,200, just to get into the starting range.

2. **Plastic jugs or pots** - You will need these for pouring and mixing purposes. It is obviously better to aim for plastic jugs for two very good reasons:

   a. They are cheaper.

   b. In case you drop one of these, they will not shatter, unlike their counterparts.

3. **Infrared thermometer** - We are all familiar with these by now, especially considering the entire pandemic situation that we just managed to survive. You will need infrared thermometers to check on the temperature of the wax and other melted items. Using a traditional thermometer will cause you to have a sticky thermometer, and any layer of wax on the thermometer might get in the way of gaining an accurate reading.

4. **Pipettes for measuring liquids** - They will come in great use.

5. **A good number of disposable gloves**

6. **Powerboards**

7. **Extension cords**

8. **A couple of fire blankets** - Safety is always the top priority when working.

9. **Fire extinguisher** - You will need to ensure that you have a fire extinguisher that is in a workable condition and is always maintained, refilled, and inspected regularly.

10. **Table covers** - Trust me, you will need all the table covers you can gather. Your table covers will start to get dirty sooner than you can imagine. Your table should remain spotless. Even the tiniest amount of dirt can quickly be submerged into the candle, and that can effectively ruin the overall quality of your final product.

11. **Digital scales** - While you can always use the traditional ones, their digital counterparts are much easier to use, and they can provide you with accurate readings without you having to do the math yourself.

12. **Silicone molds** - These are used for your melted wax. You can also go for clamshell packs as well, if that is something you prefer instead of silicone molds.

13. **Stirring spoons** - You will be doing quite a lot of stirring. Naturally, you might be compelled to buy wooden spoons, but before you do so, know that wooden spoons will immediately backfire. The molten wax will stick to the wooden handle and eventually turn into gunk that will be really hard to scrape off. Besides, wooden spoons have absorbing properties, meaning that any fragrances you use or any colors you may mix,

the wood will absorb most of it. Stick to a plastic one.

14. **Cloths** - These will be needed to handle all the pots.

15. **Templates** for wick centering

16. **Wick trimmers**

17. **Wick sizing templates**

18. **Paper towels**

19. **Metal scoops** - These are ideal for wax.

20. **Pliers** - To crimp containers

21. A **waste bin** (Katsis, 2016)

That is quite a list. It will be an extensive shopping trip, but you should get started on this as soon as you can. Time is of the essence, and delays may cause some of these items to run short in supply or be declared obsolete. It is essential for us to remain up-to-date with all the tools, equipment, and supplies needed to make the candle making business a success.

Candle Making Supplies

This list largely depends on the kind of candles you aim to produce. Depending on the niche you are interested in, you can change some of the components within this list and replace them with items or supplies which would suit your case better.

To give you a good idea, here is a list of the supplies you would typically need to start making candles on your own.

- **Jars**

- **Tea light cups** - It is best if you stick to polycarbonate, aluminum, or glass types.

- **Wax** - Always ensure that you check the wax description before going on to buy a large quantity of it.

- **Wicks** - Aim for primed wicks.

- **Color chips/Liquid concentrates**

- **Fragrances of your choice**

- **Safety stickers** - A lot of people tend to overlook tiny details. These details, including the safety stickers, matter a lot to consumers. It further enhances the trust of your customers, and it allows them to know that you care about their safety.

- **Sustainers**

- **Containers** - These include jars and teacups made of copper, marble, ceramic, and some other materials.

Some Additional Things to Know

When you begin your process of candle making, you will need to ensure you have your essential tools and supplies lined up in an organized fashion. It is very easy to lose track of things, and of time as well. You may end up running into troubling situations later on.

To avoid difficulties and prevent damage to the workspace and the house/residence in general, here are some other things you should always keep in mind.

Drainage

Right when I was starting, I would generally resort to draining away the wax. Initially, everything was going

36

perfectly well. I often wondered if I could drain the excess wax away, why should I bring home a bucket or a waste bin? I was wrong, and I learned it the hard way.

Unknown to me, the wax was molten when I drained it, but as soon as it came into contact with drain water, it changed temperature and solidified. It clogged up the drainage, and soon I had gallons of water and wax unable to go anywhere. It was disgusting to look at, and I knew I made a mistake.

I had to call in a plumber and I assure you, it was one of the most expensive repair jobs in recent times. From that day on, I have not cared whether a bucket or two occupies some space. It is perfectly okay, because it is saving me thousands of dollars.

Always ensure that you use a bucket to tackle the waste material. Never drain it. Otherwise, you too will have a hefty bill and massive financial debt.

Workspace

It is always a nice idea to cover your workbench with either aluminum foil or wax paper. This allows you to effortlessly and easily peel off any amount of spilled wax without worrying about damaging the workbench itself.

If by any chance, you are using a kitchen table, it is always a good idea to lay a towel over it. This will prevent your jars from getting cold.

Safety

Since you are working with candles, wicks, and some other components which may be flammable in nature, always ensure that you work as safely as possible.

Do not line up naked flames and flammables near each other. Also, avoid using any open or torn wires. They tend to create a spark, which is more than enough to light a fire.

With that said, it is time for you to go shopping, and then to move forward to the next chapter. In the next chapter, we will be looking into the importance of knowing the process inside out. It is indeed important, and it helps you manage things better.

I know we all would love to hire someone else to do the job, but at this phase of the business, it is best that you familiarize yourself with everything that goes in and out. Once things go in the right direction, you will then have the option of hiring someone else to carry out the jobs for you.

Chapter 3:
Know Your Process Inside Out
Part 1: Different Types of Wax and Wicks

Now that we have a good idea about the tools and supplies we need, it is time to take things up a step and get into the finer details of the entire candle making process.

When it comes to candle making, there are hundreds of variables that come into play. Everything matters, from the kind of wax you use to the fragrance you mix, all the way to the wick you prefer. Each of these elements gives you an indication of what your final product will look like. It is also important to note that choosing these individual elements can be all the difference between obtaining a quality product and one that is barely any better than the ones available within the local stores.

With that said, however, it is quite tricky to narrow down on some items, especially considering the sheer number of options you have. The same is the case with wicks and wax. There are many different forms and types of wax you can find on the market. It can quickly leave you confused, baffled, and lost. It is exactly the same when it comes to wicks. There is no "one-size-fits-all" wick in the market. You can imagine how difficult things can quickly become for someone who has no idea what kind and type of wax and wick they are looking for.

Asking the salesperson on the spot may not be the ideal thing to do either. The person may recommend a wick and a wax that does not serve you with much. It is equally possible that they may provide you with something that may be cheap, but that also may hold health and environmental hazards.

"Then how do we go about shopping for supplies?"

The only logical way is to know your process inside out, quite literally. When you develop an understanding of what you need, and you learn about all the different types, their specialties, and what purposes they are best suited for, you will have a much easier time shopping for these essential supplies.

This section is divided into two parts. The first part, which is this one, will take you through the world of wax and wicks. We will discover all about the types of wax and wicks available and which ones do what. By the end of this part, you will have a good idea of the kind of wick and wax to target. The next part, which is the next chapter, will take you through different types of candles that you can make using these supplies. You can grab a pen and a notebook to note down all the essential points. It certainly helps to have a shopping list handy.

The World of Wax

We begin with wax. To most of the people out there who have no idea about candle making, the wax is wax. To us, the people who are interested in candle making, we know that wax is a broad term. When making candles, we must know all about the variety of wax options available within the market. We should know which wax would best suit the kind of candles we aim to create. Furthermore, we must also know our targeted niche market, because the type of niche we aim to target will also change our selection of wax as well.

A certain type of wax may do wonders in one part of the market, but you may need a different type of wax to attract some other niche of the market. Depending on who you aim to target, be very cautious with the selection of your wax.

Wax is nothing more than a flammable carbon-containing solid that, as we all know, turns quickly into a liquid when burnt. Wax is essentially made using oil. Theoretically speaking, you can use almost any kind of oil to create wax. While it is an intriguing idea to be able to create your own wax, it is, however, not something we will be diving into. That is a completely different topic, and is quite time-consuming. Instead, we will stick with the premade wax, which is readily available in stores and through wholesalers.

There are many different types of wax you can find these days. You can find synthetic wax, and you can also find organic types as well. Then there are some which are a bit of a mix of the two. The options, therefore, are increasing. What we are interested in is the fact that each of these has different properties and different qualities, and each one of them brings its respective pros and cons.

This makes the entire selection of wax a little tricky. Many major candle making businesses are very picky when it comes to choosing the kind of wax they will be working with. Some would prefer to stick to paraffin wax, while some would opt for beeswax. You can do the same as well.

Paraffin Wax

Paraffin wax is perhaps the most common of waxes in use today. It is one of the most versatile waxes, if not the most (Fisher, 2019). Paraffin wax is further divided into several varieties, each with its specific melting point.

This allows you to use this wax to achieve a variety of results. You can use it for votives, containers, or even pillars.

Paraffin wax is the go-to choice for a majority of candle makers. This is why most of the candles you find in the stores are made up of paraffin wax. It is the cheapest option by a country mile, and it is hard to see why it shouldn't be.

Paraffin is a by-product of the crude oil refinement process. It is low in quality, and it is made in a large quantity. This is why it is also called mineral wax.

When it comes to paraffin wax, it is extremely good at achieving strong fragrances. It can retain the fragrance you use when making the candle for long durations. Where other forms of wax would lose the fragrance in a short period, the paraffin wax continues to release fragrance at a well-controlled rate. Apart from that, paraffin is also good at retaining its color, which is why candles made from this wax continue to remain the same in color, with virtually no sign of losing any of it.

With that said, there is a problem, and a big one at that. While the above does sound extremely compelling, especially the price part, paraffin wax hides a well-known issue behind its versatile look. When burned, the wax releases Volatile Organic Compounds (VOCs). These are considered harmful to the environment, and to us human beings if inhaled in excess. Naturally, this means that burning a lot of paraffin can actually end up harming the already suffering environment, and it can prove to be health threatening.

Therefore, it is of little surprise that paraffin wax does not enjoy a healthy reputation these days. A lot of candle makers are switching from paraffin to other synthetic or organic forms of waxes.

Soy Wax

Next in the line of wax types is the revered soy wax. This is one of the newer wax forms, invented in the early 1990s. As the name suggests, this form of wax is organic in nature. It was developed as an organic alternative for paraffin wax.

While many would point out that this form of wax is relatively young, the fact is that this type of wax has gone on to bend the rules, and it now stands as one of the most demanded waxes today.

As time progresses, the demand for organic and natural candles is rising, and it is a strong indicator that people are growing more and more conscious about their choices and how they affect the environment. With the entire "save the planet" drive outperforming, outliving, and surpassing all expectations, it is safe to assume that organic materials will continue to be in high demand for years to come, and this is why candles made from soy wax are such a success.

Candles made using this wax burn cleanly, meaning they do not emit any harmful vapors at all. The wax is made from soybeans. It is considered to have the longest burning time of all the waxes. Just like its petroleum wax counterpart, soy wax also has a variety of melting points and blends. Some are 100% soy wax, some are blended together with other vegetable oils such as coconut oil, and then there are some which are infused together with paraffin on a 51% soy, 49% paraffin ratio. The last one is also called a soy wax blend.

"Well, this certainly seems to be a more logical option."

Once again, you might be rushing into making a decision. Soy wax is more expensive, albeit not the most expensive. That title goes to another form of wax, which we will be discussing shortly.

Truthfully, the only downside of this wax is the price tag. If you are able to look past that or find the prices manageable, it is worthy of your time and consideration.

Candle Gel Wax

Right away, let me clear up one thing. Candle gel wax is not wax at all. Yes, you read that right.

The fact is that gel wax, as it is popularly known, is a blend of mineral oils and resins. This may come to you as a bit of a surprise, but the Penreco company actually patents the famous gel wax. That would mean that the gel wax you are using most likely came from their company.

The beauty of gel wax is the fact that the wax (let's call it that) is transparent and clear. This allows candle makers to mix in all types of flowers and petals to give their candles an artistic feel. Throw in a few drops of fragrance, and what you end up with is an exotic candle, ready to mesmerize onlookers and end-users.

It is very good at holding both colors and scents. There are a few types of gel wax you may come across, and the only difference between these types will be the clarity or transparency. Some may be as clear as water, while some may have a hint of shade. Both can be used to create unique candles, and it all depends on the type of product you intend to create. It is a worthy competitor, especially if you are looking to create novelty candle designs, replicating the colors and textures of water, beer, or wine.

Gel wax is also available in a firm form, meaning you can use the gel wax for crafting pillar candles. It all sounds lovely, right? There is, however, one big issue to consider. It uses the same petroleum substance found in paraffin wax, and that means that you cannot expect it to be completely clean when it burns. Apart from that, it is a good choice, especially considering the artistic nature of the wax itself.

Beeswax

When it comes to waxes, beeswax is known as the oldest wax form in existence. It is made naturally by honeybees as a byproduct in the honey-making process.

This special type of wax is so old that beeswax candles were found in the pyramids, suggesting that beeswax was used even then.

The wax is obtained through the combs, which is excreted by the bees to incubate their larvae. Due to the fact that it is infused with honey, it contains a naturally sweet fragrance. The fragrance may vary, depending on the type of flowers the bees have been feeding on.

After harvesting the beeswax, it is melted and then filtered a few times. It is then given a final shape of blocks or slabs, which are then sold to the market as beeswax. Both of these melt very easily, and some can also be sold in pre-rolled sheets as well. If you intend to buy these sheets, you will not need to melt the wax to create your candles at all.

Since it is a natural and organic product, it burns clean and does not pollute the air at all. For the same reason, the scent, when compared to its synthetic counterparts, is less noticeable. It is also important to point out that it cannot be mixed with other fragrances, so if you end up buying this, you do not have the choice to go for a different fragrance. However, the biggest issue of them all is its price.

Remember how I mentioned earlier that one wax type holds the distinct honor of being the most expensive one on the market? Well, you are reading about it right now. Beeswax is the most expensive alternative of them all.

Palm Wax

This type of wax is quite similar to the soy wax we learned about earlier. Just like soy wax, palm wax is also made from its respective oil. Palm wax is perhaps one of the firmest waxes in existence, firm enough to be almost brittle. It is highly effective if you are looking to create votive or pillar candles.

If you have come across candles that have a feathered effect or a kind of a crystalline texture, you are looking at a candle that was made using palm wax.

You can also browse around to find even firmer palm wax blends. There are some which are mixed with soy wax, and the result is a wax blend that is quite firm in nature.

It is all-natural, meaning that it will not harm you or the atmosphere when it is burned. It is also well priced, and allows you to experience almost the same benefits as soy wax.

There are many other types of waxes, but most of them combine a wax or two to create new blends. You can experiment with such blends on your own, but these are generally the ones that are widely used, and they provide satisfactory results. Now comes the time to answer yet another burning question:

"Which one should I choose?"

Well, that is an easy one, as we shall see in the next section of the book.

Choosing the Best Type of Wax

Now that you have some idea about the types of waxes, you should come to know which type of wax is best suited for what kind of candle. If you feel lost or you do not know what a specific type of candle looks and feels like, you can always search it on the internet. Alternatively, you can take a quick look at one of your local stores to see the candle type personally and get a chance to inspect it closer. It should provide you with a good idea of what you can expect the results to be, and then you can decide which type of candle suits you best.

Votive Candles

Votive candles are easily recognizable. They are commonly used for prayer stations and in the churches, and are often seen in the movies as well. They are short and thick in shape, typically white in color. They are also seen within many houses as a part of their decorations.

Votive candles, considering their shape, can be made using a variety of waxes. However, the ideal ones to use are:

- Soy Wax
- Paraffin Wax
- Soy Wax Blend (Soy/Paraffin)
- Palm Wax
- Beeswax
- Gel Wax

Dipped Candles

Dipped candles are quite different. Unlike the previous type, they are thin, long, and cylindrical. They are made by dipping the wick repeatedly in melted tallow.

Since these are different in structure and feel, the best waxes to use for them are:

- Paraffin Wax
- Beeswax

Anything other than that, and you might not be able to achieve the right results.

Container Candles/Tealight Candles

These are the type of candles you would normally see in spas, romantic settings in movies, and often floating on top of the water for special occasions. These are made in thin metal or plastic cups, allowing the entire candle to liquefy when they are burned.

To make these little candles, you can use a variety of waxes. Well, when I say variety, I literally mean all the types I mentioned above.

Pillar Candles

Just as the name suggests, these candles are shaped like pillars. They are made using wax and fatty substances, giving them their popular texture and shape.

To create pillar candles, you can use the following waxes:

- Paraffin wax
- Beeswax
- Palm wax
- Wax blends

48

You cannot use the gel wax or the soy wax for these.

Rolled Candles

These are quite literally rolled, thus the name 'rolled' candles. Owing to their unique design, they are only made using beeswax. No other form of wax is available in pre-rolled sheets.

These are some of the most popular options in existence today. Depending on the type of candle you aim to produce, you can set your sights for their respective waxes and buy the supplies according to your needs.

All About Wicks

By now, you should have a good idea of the variety of waxes available on the market today. It is also possible that you might have already decided to go for a wax or a blend, and that is a good thing. As long as you are confident you can produce quality goods, you can stick with your decision. Should you have any doubts, you can always pause briefly and rethink your plans.

Now that we know all about waxes, it is time to focus our attention on the other important aspect of candles: the wicks.

Generally speaking, a lot of candle makers overlook the importance of choosing the right wick. Once again, to many who may not have any prior experience or knowledge about candle making, wicks would just be pieces of thread that are primed together. However, the reality is a little different.

Yes, they all serve the same purpose, and that is to burn. But did you know that even the slightest drop in quality can leave you with a wick that is either hard to burn, or one that burns right through? That is possible, which is why you must know your wicks as well. It will further help you understand which wicks are ideal for the kind of project you are pursuing.

The main job of a wick is to provide fuel to the fire to burn. Since it is acting as a fuel source, its quality matters. If the wick is too thick or too thin, you could either end up with a wick that cannot sustain a fire or one that would burn like a flare.

Today, there are well over a hundred types of wicks within the market, and that is a problem. If you are someone who has no idea what you are looking for, it is recommended that you first find out all about the popular types of wicks, and then come to a decision on which type of wick you intend to use. Choosing the right type of wick is important because it will either make your product burn nicely, burn quickly, or lose the ability to burn smoothly.

Categories of Wicks

The majority of the wick types on the market are made using braided, knitted or plaited fibers. This encourages a slow but steady burn. Wicks that are twisted are lower in quality as opposed to ones that are braided or knitted. Twisted wicks burn at a faster pace, owing to their loose construction. They end up allowing more fuel to reach the fire, hence burning through the entire candle at a much faster pace.

With that said, twisted wicks are actually very useful when it comes to creating candles for birthdays or anniversaries.

Regardless of their construction type, wicks are grouped into a few categories. Each of these categories differs from one another. All of these use some of the types mentioned above of wick constructions.

Flat Wicks

These can be flat-plaited or, at times, knitted. They are generally made using three bundles of fiber. They are quite consistent when it comes to burning, and because of their unique construction, they curl in the flame, providing a self-trimming effect (National Candle Association, n.d.).

Of all the wick types you will come across, these are the most commonly used. You can find these in tapers and pillar candles, and some other candles as well.

Square Wicks

Quite like the flat wicks, these braided, or sometimes knitted, wicks also provide the same self-trimming effect, meaning that they curl in the flame. However, unlike the flat wicks, they are more rounded and slightly more robust. They are highly recommended for candles using beeswax. This is due to the fact that this type of wick can prevent wick clogging.

Wick clogging occurs with specific types of wax formulations, fragrances, or pigments. By using this type of wick, you can rule that issue out right away.

Cored Wicks

This is yet another type of braided or knitted wick. This type of wick, however, has a uniquely constructed design. It uses a core material, which in turn ensures that the wick remains straight and is upright when burning.

Cored wicks come with round cross-sections. It is also to be noted that using different materials for the core provides the user with a variety of stiffness effects. For the core, the most common materials you can find include:

51

- Paper
- Cotton
- Tin
- Zinc

You can find this type of wick used in pillar candles, jar candles, votives, and some other devotional lights as well.

Wooden Wicks

Now, these are exquisite and quite popular these days. The main reason behind their popularity is the fact that they tend to create visual aesthetics that are pleasing to the eyes. Not to forget, they also make small and soft crackling noises when they burn.

You can find wooden wicks in single-ply, curved, multi-layered, and some decorative shapes. They are usually made from 100% wood, but there are some which are made of semi-wood, fibrous material, or at times a combination of cotton and wood.

They are very popular, and you can certainly use them to create unique candles for special occasions.

Specialty Wicks

Apart from the ones we have come across above, there are some wicks that are made for special purposes. They are explicitly designed to "meet the burn characteristics of specific candle applications, such as oil lamps and insect-repelling candles." (National Candle Association, n.d.).

HTP Wicks

These are also known as high-tension paper wicks. This special type of wick combines the best of two worlds: the self-trimming effect, plus the rigid structure of core wicks. The results are equally impressive. These reinforced wicks can provide an improved wax pool symmetry while reducing carbon heading (also known as mushrooming). They are an excellent choice to go for if you are looking to use:

- Paraffin wax

- Vegetable wax

- Soy wax

- Penreco gel wax

Performa Coreless Wick

This is a specialized flat braided wick made using only cotton. Because of the way these are engineered, they do not bend when burning. This means that the wick will remain straight throughout its life. They are also a good option if you are looking for wicks that can produce a more robust flame, especially when used with more viscous applications.

LX Wicks

This is yet another special type of wick that is braided, flat, and most importantly, coreless. They are manufactured using stable threads to ensure an optimum burning profile. Despite the fact that they are made uniquely, they still do tend to bend a little as they burn, and that ensures that the wick has a consistent and stable burn.

This wick also minimizes carbon buildup, or mushrooming, and it also reduces soot, smoke, and afterglow. If you are looking to work with container and pillar candles, these are a very good alternative. They are best used with:

- Paraffin Wax
- Soy Wax
- Vegetable Waxes

RRD Series Wick

This type of wick comes from the same people who produce the LX series wicks. They are round, braided, and cotton cored candle wicks, providing increased fuel flow to the flame (both wax and fragrance).

These types of wicks are excellent because they do not clog or drown in the melted wax, making them a perfect choice for candle makers who aim to create container and votive candles. Since they are able to provide an increased flow of fuel, you can also use them to pack in some extra fragrance to make the overall experience even better.

Burning with a slight curl, these are highly dependable and stable, and provide a consistent burn.

CD Series Wick

This type of wick is yet another coreless wick. However, unlike the ones before, these ones are non-directional and flat braided. They are identifiable by the special paper filament that is woven around them.

This wick is designed to ensure a consistent and maximum burn. It is quite versatile, and it works very well with waxes, which are harder to melt.

Knowing Wick Sizes

Of course, the biggest hurdle isn't the type of wick you will be using. Instead, it is the size of the wick you need. To fully understand this, you must first know the ideal sizes of the candles you are aiming to produce. Then, you can use those figures to have a fair idea of how much of a wick you will require.

Do not worry if you have no idea or have not yet measured the candles yourself. Below, you will find a table that takes you through all the measurements accordingly. It should give you a fair idea of what you should be looking for, what the ideal size of the wick would be (per candle), and a few other important pieces of information.

Please note that the table below is more of a recommended size chart. You may still need to adjust the length of the wick or the candle you are producing accordingly.

Candle Size	Wick Type	Type of Wax	Tab	Wick Coating
1 – ⅛"	28 - 24 Zinc	Paraffin	15 mm	High Melting Point
1 – ⅛"	S330	Paraffin	15 mm	High Melting Point
1 – ⅛"	TL 25/S - 30 nst 2	Versa gel	15 x 6 mm	210 degrees
1 – ⅛"	TL 18/S - 30 nst 2	Veggie Waxes	15 mm	High Melting Point

Table One: Tea-light Candles (Using Paraffin, Versa Gel, and Veggie Waxes)

Candle Size	Type of Wax	Wick Type
6 x 6" (3 wicks)	Paraffin and Veggie Waxes	15 ply vRRD-29 nst 2
2 - 3" (Small)		LX-14 RRD-37 nst 2
3" (Medium)		LX-16 RRD-40 nst 2
4" (Large)		LX-20 RRD-47 nst 2

Table Two: Pillar Candles

Candle Size	Wick Type	Type of Wax	Tab	Wick Coating

2.5"	LX-10	Paraffin	20 mm	High Melting Point
2.5"	36-24-24 Zinc	Paraffin	33 mm	High Melting Point
2.5"	RRD-34 nst 2	Veggie Waxes	20 mm	High Melting Point

Table Three: Votive Candles

Candle Size	Wick Type	Type of Wax	Tab	Wick Coating
1-2" (Small)	CD-3	Versa Gel	20 x 9 mm	210 degrees
1-2" (Small)	RRD-29 nst 2	Veggie Waxes	20 mm	High Melting Point
1-2" (Small)	34-40 Zinc	Paraffin	20 mm	High Melting Point
2-3" (Medium)	HZL 38 C	Versa Gel	20 x 9 mm	210 degrees
2-3" (Medium)	RRD-40 nst 2	Veggie Waxes	20 mm	High Melting Point
2-3" (Medium)	LX-14	Paraffin	20 mm	High Melting Point

3-4" (Large)	HTP-105	Versa Gel	20 x 9 mm	210 degrees
3-4" (Large)	RRD-47 nst 2	Veggie Waxes	20 mm	High Melting Point
3-4" (Large)	CD-16	Paraffin	20 mm	High Melting Point
4+" (XL)	(2) RRD-37 nst 2	Veggie Waxes	20 mm	High Melting Point
4+" (XL)	60-44-18 Cotton	Paraffin	20 mm	High Melting Point

Table Four: Container Candles

It is important to note that if you intend to use one-pour paraffin wax, you might have to go up by a size or two from the ones recommended above.

This brings our journey into wax and wicks to an end, at least for now. In the next chapter, we will see the next part of *Know Your Process Inside Out*. That is where we will be discussing the different types of candles. You already know about some, but in the next chapter, we will be diving into the details to gain a better understanding of what defines a specific type of candle, and how we can learn to identify which ones are which. This will be quite helpful, especially considering that you may opt to produce more than a single type of candle. The more you know, the better you can research regarding niche markets, and whether or not the product you intend to produce is in demand.

58

To make things a little easier, I will provide you with a detailed guide on how to create said types of candles. It is fun, it is intuitive, and it is undoubtedly something a candlemaker should be able to do.

Chapter 4:
Know Your Process Inside Out
Part 2: Different Types of
Candles

In the previous chapter, we learned a great deal about the various types of waxes available on the market. We gained a fair insight into what makes them suitable, what type of waxes mass producers use, and why. We also learned some valuable information about the kinds of wicks used with said waxes. It is easy to see why both of these play a vital part in the making of our candles. After all, a candle is simply impossible to create if you take away either of these things.

With that said, it is now time to dive into the world of candles, more specifically, the types that are known, produced, and popular within the industry. This chapter will take you through a variety of candle types that you can choose to work upon. It is imperative to know the kind of candle you are choosing to produce and to learn all about it. This will further allow you to understand and identify what is right and what isn't. It will also help you to ensure you buy the right kind of supplies and tools to get the job done easily and effectively.

Finally, with each type that we will learn about, we will also learn how to make them. After all, what fun is there if we cannot make them? This might be a good time to grab a pen and a few papers to note down the steps. You will need to memorize each one of them in their respective order to ensure you not only learn how to create candles, but master the art as well. Once you know how to make these candles, you can then go on a creative spree to design and modify the look and feel of the candle as per your desire.

Making the Candles

You may already know a candle type or two. It is also possible that you may already have an idea of the kind of candle you will be hoping to produce and sell as a part of your successful business, and all that is good. The trouble is, people often venture out to create an array of designs and types without realizing that diversifying their lineup at such a critical phase can jeopardize their chances of success.

Think about it: if you go on to create four, five, or even six different candle types at the start, you might need to spend extra to buy supplies for six different products. Some of the supplies may be universal, meaning that you can use them to create any type of candle, but some candle types need very specific components. That would only increase your cost.

As a suggestion from a person who once found himself in the same situation, stick to one or two types at most at first. Perfect them, get the response you need, and then think about expanding your lineup.

This decision can, therefore, only be made once you know which candle types are a must to go for, and whether or not there exists a better type that you can make. As we walk through each type of candle, see which one catches your attention the most. You can then try and practice making such candles on your own before adding it to the lineup of your business. With that said, let us explore the numerous types of candles.

Votive Candles

One of the most famous candles today is the votive candle. This type of candle is often used to improve the ambiance of a place. Given their properties, they add warmth to any given setting. They are extremely easy to create, and they are easy to customize as well.

You can use these to set the right tone for your next event, celebration, or anniversary. All you need to do is change the color to match the appropriate occasion. To give it that exquisite final touch, use a fragrance of your choice, and let the votive candle do the rest for you.

If you have been making votive candles, you will know that these are not meant to stand on their own (freestanding). The process of creating these candles is easy and quite similar to the process for pillar candles, which we will look into later. When it comes to burning, they act more like container candles and provide glow and consistency of a similar level.

When creating votive candles, you will need to ensure that you use holders that are explicitly rated for votive candles. You can find many in stores readily available, so choosing one will not be a problem.

Depending on the wax you use, you may need to do a second pour the following day. The one we are about to create will be using seafoam dye blocks, as well as a sea mist fragrance oil. You can search for these easily online, or simply ask at your local store.

The Materials

To create a votive candle, we will be using the following:

- Small pouring pitcher
- LX-14 6" Pre Tabbed Wick 100-piece bag

- Infrared thermometer
- Candle + soap scale
- Flared votive candle mold 10-piece pack
- Votive blend wax 10 lbs. slab
- Votive wick pin 10-piece bag
- 3 oz. standard votive holder 36-piece case
- Seafoam dye blocks 1-piece bag
- Sea mist 4 oz. bottle

Some additional items that you may require include:

- Double boiler
- Rubbing Alcohol
- Paper cups
- Markers
- Paper towels
- Spatula, or any kind of large spoon

The Method

This method will be divided into four steps.

Step One

The first and foremost thing to do is to prepare your workspace and the supplies you will use.

Clear out any excessive clutter on your workstation. You will need to have a clean and organized workstation to ensure you can get the job done right and without any issues.

Using a scale, measure one pound of the votive blend wax and set it aside. Using the same scale, now weigh 1 oz. of sea mist fragrance oil, then set it aside as well.

Next, we will prepare our votive molds using a clean paper towel and a little bit of rubbing alcohol. The idea is to clean them from the inside and wipe out any dust or debris.

Caution: You will need to be a bit careful when cleaning and wiping out the votive molds. They have very sharp edges and can easily cut into the skin.

After cleaning the molds, place one wick pin in the center of each of your votive molds. With these prepared, it is time to start phase two of the process.

Step Two

In this phase, we will be melting the wax and using fragrance.

Using a double boiler, place the one pound of wax you set aside earlier into the boiler and allow it to melt. If you are unable to fit the one-pound block in, you can cut it down to shorter pieces and place them inside the boiler.

As the wax continues to melt, start breaking off the seafoam dye block to use with your votives. It is recommended that you use only one-fourth of the block for every pound of wax you use. This is not a rule of thumb, but for this specific project, I used this much. You still have the option of changing the size of the block you use or how much of it you use, depending on the shade you wish to achieve in the end.

By now, the wax should have fully melted. If so, it is time for you to mix in the dye block pieces we broke off earlier. Stir gently as you continue to add the block pieces. You will know when to stop when the blocks have dispersed the colors entirely and mixed equally throughout the molten wax.

With a thermometer, check the temperature. If the temperature has reached 185 ° F, you can continue forward to add the fragrance you previously measured and set aside. Once the fragrance is added, remove the boiler from heat and continue stirring gently for the next two or three minutes as it cools off.

Step Three

Keep checking the temperature because as soon as it cools down to 175 °F, we will initiate our first pour.

Here, you need to ensure you do not pour the wax immediately. You will need to pour the wax into the molds slowly and carefully. Fill the wax all the way up to the lip of the mold, then do the same for the rest of the molds you have lined up with their wicks.

Let the votives cool down for the rest of the day. As they do so, they will start to shrink. This is why we will need to do a second pour the next day, to fill out the space left by the shrunken wax.

For the remaining wax, pour it in a paper cup. Use more paper cups, if needed. After doing so, ensure that you use a marker and write down the following details on each of these cups containing the remaining wax:

- *Type of wax*
- *Fragrance used*
- *Date of batch*

In our case, it should be votive blend wax, sea mist, and today's date. We will use these tomorrow to refill the space created after the wax has settled and shrunk.

The next day, simply remove the paper from the paper cups and place the solid blocks of wax into the double boiler. This time, however, heat the wax until it reaches

190 °F. This is to ensure that the solidified and cooled votive melts easily and adjusts itself accordingly.

Once the wax has reached the optimum temperature, carefully pour it in the votive molds, ensuring you cover any sinkholes created overnight. Once again, you will need to fill it to the lip of the mold. Once done, allow the votive molds to cool off completely.

Step Four

The fourth and final phase will begin once the votive is completely cooled off and solidified. Begin by removing the votives from their molds. You will need to simply pull on the wick pin gently until the entire block comes out nicely.

Tip: In most cases, the votive should be easily pulled out, without any resistance. However, in some cases you may feel like it is stuck or needs a harder pull. Instead of pulling it harder, place it in a refrigerator for just a few minutes. This will allow the solidified wax to further contract in size, hence allowing you to pull the candle out nice and easy.

Now that you have removed the candle from the mold, place the mold aside. Flip the candle over and push the top of the wick pin in firmly. Once the base plate of the wick pin lifts up, pull it out. It is imperative that you do not do this on a kind of surface that could be, or is, damaged.

Now, replace each of the wick pins with the LX-14 pre tabbed wicks. Place each wick in the base of the wick pin, and let the wick go through from the bottom to the top of the candle. Once set, cut them off from the top to one-fourth of an inch.

Now, all that remains is to light them up and enjoy a wonderfully refreshing candle that not only burns consistently, but looks good and smells incredible. However, don't rush just yet. We aren't entirely done, if I am being honest. You still need to do one more thing.

Place the candles into the votive approved holders. For safety instructions, place a safety label at the bottom of the holder. This should effectively leave you with a fresh new batch of votive candles.

Dipped Candles

These candles are exquisite to look at and are artistic in nature. They are long, cylindrical, tube-like candles that have a narrowing snout at the top. They are generally seen in an array of colors. They are also known as dipped tapers.

These are made primarily using beeswax and paraffin wax. With that said, you can also use soy wax to create dipped tapers. However, should you intend to do that, it is good to know that the soy wax will need a longer set up time between the layers. For this example, you can work with either the beeswax or the paraffin wax.

The reason why beeswax is used more commonly to create these tapers is the fact that melted beeswax is more viscous. This means that you will need to do less 'dipping', as compared to paraffin wax. You may only need to dip it between seven to 10 times, whereas for the paraffin, you will need to dip twice as much. It is also to be noted that the beeswax tapers burn a little longer, as opposed to their paraffin counterparts.

In case you are someone who is on a tighter budget, you can always opt to use paraffin as your choice of wax. It will take a lot more dipping than the beeswax to achieve the kind of thickness you are looking for. However, you can rest assured that you will still end up with exquisite results using paraffin. For paraffin users, it is preferred that you use straight paraffin with a medium or high melting point. Some types of paraffin wax melt at lower temperatures, so those are the kind you should avoid.

You can find some types of paraffin wax with medium melting points, and should be able to take advantage of the hardening additives. These would give your tapers a more rigid look and feel. One of the most common hardening additives found in paraffin wax is called stearic acid, also known as stearine. Whatever you choose between the beeswax or the paraffin, you can achieve the desired results.

The Materials

To create the dipped candles, you will need:

- Beeswax or paraffin
- Double boiler
- Wick of your choice
- Wick pins
- Thermometer
- Cold water
- A broom
- Mat knife

You do not need any additional items to make dipped candles.

The Method

Step One

Start by setting up your double boiler, then place the wax of your choice in it to start the melting process. Once the wax is melted, transfer it into a pot. You will need to use a tall pot, ideally of the height you wish your candles to achieve. You can place this pot in a stockpot that is half-full of water. Place the stockpot over high heat.

With a thermometer, keep checking the temperature and ensure that it remains under 200 degrees. Ideally, the working temperature should be around 165 degrees.

Step Two

This step is a bit tricky, but with a bit of practice, you should soon be able to do this relatively easy.

You will need to create a rig that can hold the length of the wick. Depending on the size of your taper, you will need to use a wick twice the length of the taper. This is necessary because you will need to dip your tapers in pairs. Ensure that you do not make your tapers taller than the dipping vat you are using.

Step Three

You will also need to tie some weights at the wick ends. For that, you can use metal nut fishing weights, or even a few coins stuck together (use a bit of wax). The weights are used to ensure that the wicks are held straight and are taut. Do not worry, as you will be cutting these off around halfway through the process.

Once your wicks have started to accumulate some wax, they will remain straight on their own.

Step Four

Start dipping your tapers. You can continue to repeat the process until you have acquired the desired thickness. You will need to allow several minutes for the layers to cool off before you apply another one on them. If you do not allow these layers to cool off properly, the wax will start to fall off the wick.

Ensure that the dipping motion is continuous and smooth. You will also need to make sure that you do not pause when the tapers are submerged.

Step Five

When you have achieved around half of the thickness you desire, cut off the weights at the bottom of the tapers. Continue dipping your tapers a few more times. After having reached the desired thickness, just hang your tapers and let them dry.

Note: Always make sure that you use a scale and measure out the thickness/diameter of the taper holders, and then measure the thickness of your tapers to ensure the correct thickness is achieved.

It is a good practice to leave your newly created tapers to hang as a pair. It is easier for storage purposes, and each taper acts as a counterbalance to the other, allowing both to remain steady and straight. Once they have cooled off, simply cut the connecting wick and use them as you please.

Container Candles

In essence, the container candle is nothing more than a non-flammable container that is filled using wax and has a wick. They are considered a popular choice for people, especially given their unique shapes and designs. They do not drip at all, which is unlike any other candle. That is because the container prevents the excess wax from flowing out.

Since these are contained in a container, a lower melting point wick can easily be used. This is beneficial if you are aiming to enhance the fragrance of the candle as it burns. It is safe to say that container candles, unlike their freestanding counterparts, are the best when it comes to throwing their scent around.

These are elegant to look at and stylish, and can easily be stored. Apart from the fact that the containers are normally made using glass, there isn't much about them that could go wrong.

The Materials

To make these delightful little candles, you will need:

- The wax of your choice - Ensure that the wax you choose is suitable for containers
- Other desired additives of your choice, such as fragrance oils and dyes
- Containers - These must be suitable for candles
- Double boiler
- Pre-tabbed wicks - The size should be ideal for the container you intend to use
- Hot glue - Use a glue gun, if possible
- Bic Pen
- Thermometer
- Heat gun
- Clothespins

The Method

This method is also divided in steps.

Step 1

Place the wax you intend to use in the double boiler and allow it to melt. You should be able to read these instructions as your wax continues to melt away.

Be sure that you attain a good temperature range, ideally between 170 to 175 degrees. Once the wax has melted completely, you can go on to add any additives of your choice to the wax. Mix the wax and the additives thoroughly. To make things easier, add them in the following order:

1. Additives, such as stearic acid or vybar - If you are using the IGI-4786 wax, you will not need to use these.

2. Fragrance oil

3. The dye of your choice

The above is done to provide you with a visual confirmation that all your mixtures have mixed well enough with the wax.

As your wax continues to melt, continue with the next few steps. However, be sure to keep an eye on the melting wax and check it every now and then to ensure it is holding the right temperature.

Step Two

It is time to add the wicks to the containers you will be using for your container candles. Grab a bic pen and disassemble it. Yes, you read that right. You will need the barrel of the pen. The rest can be discarded.

Straighten out the pre-tabbed wicks you are using. You do not have to make them be perfectly straight, but straightening them out enough so that they form a slight curve is good enough.

Now, insert the straightened out pre-tabbed wick through the barrel you just made from the bic pen. The six-inch wicks are perfect for this job. By having the wick pass through the barrel, you will make handling the wick a lot easier for yourself as you proceed with the rest of the steps.

Right about now, you will need to use some hot glue or a glue gun and apply the hot glue on the base of the wick tab you will be using. This must be done while holding the wick within the barrel. Do not pull it out.

Using the barrel to guide your wick, place the base tab of the wick pin in the center of the container and press hard on it to ensure it sticks to the center. Once the base tab is stuck to the middle of the container, simply remove the barrel by sliding it off.

Step Three

Obviously, the wick will fall to the side as soon as you slide the barrel off. This means we need to use something to hold it taut and in its place. For this, we will be using a clothespin.

Using the clothespin, secure the top of the wick and place the clothespin on the lips of the container. It should be placed in the center so that the wick is taut, straight, and does not fall loose. If you have a larger container, you may need to improvise a little.

For larger containers, one good way to secure the top of the wick is to loop the wick around a wooden skewer.

Step Four

In the fourth phase, you will need to preheat the container itself. It is also worth noting that this step is optional, but if you wish to achieve a better-finished product, this step will certainly help you.

Once the wax reaches the proper working temperature, preheat your container with a heat gun. You will need to preheat it to about 150 degrees. If you do not have a heat gun, you can always use an oven by using the lowest heat settings.

Important: If you are using a heat gun, you should take care, as the heat gun can quickly go above 150 degrees.

Step Five

Next, we will start with our initial pour. Before pouring, make sure you check the temperature. It should not be less than 160 degrees.

Carefully fill up the container. You can either fill it to the lip of the container, or you can fill it to the desired height. If you are using a container that has a lid on it, be sure to fill it to a certain extent so that it does not obstruct the lid, and still leaves enough room for the lid to open or close and fit back into its position.

For the remainder of the wax, which may be around 20% or so, pour it into paper cups. Once again, label your paper cups with the date, type of wax used, and any additives used, and then set it aside to cool.

Set aside the container with the wax to cool as well. Generally, it will take around six hours, but if you have added any additives, you may need slightly more time. Do not put your container into a cooling unit. Slow cooling downtime will ensure a better finish and provide optimum results.

Step Six

After the container with the wax and wick has cooled off properly, it is time to do a second pour.

Remove the paper from the paper cup and melt the wax. Once again, ensure that the temperature of the wax is around five degrees higher than before. By doing so, it increases the adhesion between all the layers of wax.

Now pour the wax, but ensure that you only pour enough so that it barely covers the surface of the wax produced by the initial pour. Do not fill it more than that. If there are any sinkholes, ensure you fill those as well.

Finally, allow the container candle to cool off properly.

Step Seven

Cut off the wick after the candle has completely cooled off. Ideally, trim the wick to one-fourth of an inch.

With that, you have just finished making your container candle. Well done!

Pillar Candles

Pillar candles are one of the most common candles seen around the market, and in houses as well. The beauty of pillar candles is the fact that they can be molded into many shapes and sizes. You can find a lot of shapes and differently sized molds for pillar candles. You can choose to stick with the traditional pillar candles, or you can make things a little more interesting and shape one like a pyramid. The choices are quite a lot to count.

You can find a variety of mold materials such as silicone, latex, plastic, and aluminum, but the biggest range of designs and shapes comes in the form of sheet metal. These molds are very durable, and you can use them for years with bare minimum maintenance.

The Materials

To create your own batch of pillar candles/shaped candles, you will need:

- Pouring pots
- Thermometer
- Wick bar - This is only required if you are using aluminum molds

- Rubber Plugs - Required only if you are using aluminum molds

- Mold Release - These are sprayed on the mold to make the extraction of the candle a lot easier

- Wax - You can choose from:
    - ☐ Soy Wax
    - ☐ Votive/pillar blend wax (search for CBL-141)
    - ☐ Mottling Wax - For pillars or votive candles

- Fragrance of your choice

- Aluminum or designer candle molds

- Dye material of your choice - Ideally, you should opt for color blocks

- Wick - You can choose one from the table below (keep the diameter in consideration)

	2" Diameter	*3" Diameter*	*4" Diameter*
4045 H	15 ply/21 ply	21 ply/24 ply	24 ply/27 ply
CBL-141	18 ply/21 ply	24 ply/27 ply	30 ply/36 ply

Types of Wicks to Choose From

The Process

Step One

Start the process by preheating your mold. This is important because a cold container will cause what is known as surface chilling, and that may not provide the desired results. The heating will make way for a smoothly finished candle.

Once the mold is preheated, you can use the barrel technique we learned earlier to set in a wick pin. If your mold comes with a separate base, you can drill a hole in it and pass the wick through it. Secure this end of the base with a screw so that the wick does not go anywhere. Use a clothespin at the lip of the container to hold the wick in position. It should be taut and straight.

Step Two

Start heating your wax in a double boiler. Heat the wax until it is completely liquefied. For this project, ensure that you check the temperature and maintain it at around 190 degrees. This is when you can add the additives, such as color blocks/dyes. If you are not using any of these additives, continue to heat up the mixture until it reaches 200 degrees.

Step Three

You can skip this step if you are not using any additives, such as colors.

When the thermometer shows a reading of 190 degrees, start adding the additives to the molten wax. Make sure that you mix the mixture thoroughly using a large wooden spoon or tool of your choice. Gently stir for a few minutes to ensure that the color is mixed properly.

Step Four

Now, start reducing the heat to bring the temperature down to around 175 degrees. Before you start the pouring process, add any fragrance now and blend it well. Adding fragrance at a higher temperature is not recommended.

Step Five

Once the additives are mixed well, it is time to start the pouring process.

Start by carefully pouring the wax mixture into the mold of your choice. Be sure that you leave just about enough room for re-pouring purposes. As the wax settles and cools off, it will shrink. To top off the candle, you will need to re-pour one more time later.

Step Six

Save the remaining wax in a paper cup or two. Make sure to label the paper cup with a marker clearly. Include the information as we have done before (date, type of wax, and additives used). Set this wax aside for the second pour and allow it to cool off.

At the same time, let the mold with the wax cool off as well. Once it has cooled off, which will take around two hours, you can continue with the re-pour.

Step Seven

After the initial pour has cooled off, reheat the remaining wax in the cup and melt it. Ensure that the temperature is correct before proceeding to re-pour. Top off the space in the mold with the reheated wax and set it aside for cooling.

You can allow the candle to cool off at room temperature. Alternatively, you can use some other methods to cool it off faster. However, faster cooling may not provide you with the ideal results.

Step Eight

Now that the mold has cooled off, it is time to take it off. You can use the silicone mold release, or the spray I mentioned earlier. You can use these after every six pours into the mold. This will ensure that the mold remains clean and does not clog up or get stuck.

Finally, remove the mold and unveil your newly created pillar/shaped candle to the world.

Rolled Candles

These are exquisite to look at, terrific fun to make, and are perhaps the easiest ones to make. Despite that, they are artistic to look at and very elegant to have in your living room. These are made only using beeswax and cannot be made with the help of any other wax.

Rolled candles produce a subtle warm glow, and they provide a wonderful scent as well. Another good thing about this type of candle comes from the fact that you do not need a melting pot for this one at all. Since these are made using beeswax sheets, the melting part is no longer required.

The Materials

To create your very own rolled candles, you will need:

- Beeswax sheets - You can generally find these in either eight-inch or 16-inch sizes
- Primed wick - One that is appropriate for a 1-inch candle
- A sharp knife
- Suitable cutting surface

The Process

Step One

Lay out a single beeswax sheet on a flat surface. On the edge of the sheet, place a wick that is at least three-fourths of an inch longer than the height of the sheet. In case you are using an eight-inch sheet, simply cut the wick to a size of eight and three-fourth inches.

Tip: It is a good idea to leave three-fourths of an inch of wick on either side of the sheet. Upon completion, whichever end looks better, you can trim the length of one side and keep the other as your top side.

Step Two

With the wick still in place, start rolling the beeswax sheet by rolling only about one-eighth of an inch. This small channel can be used to enclose and envelop the wick. As you start to roll, press down firmly to ensure that the wax is tight around the wick. Note that you only need to press down firmly during the first roll. This is to ensure the wick remains in place and is secure. After this, you no longer need to press down firmly.

Continue working from one end all the way to the other. Roll slowly and gently.

Ensure that the turning and bending process does not alter the shape. It should be smoothly done and kept as straight as possible for better visual aesthetics.

Step Three

Once you are at the end of the roll, you can opt to add another sheet of beeswax to give your candle a thicker look. If you intend to stick with one, press down gently on the final edge, all the way to the sides of the candle. You should be able to form a smooth edge.

Step Four

Choose which end looks better as the top. With your top selected, trim the wick if needed at the top, and cut off the one at the bottom.

Bonus Tips

Since we are talking about the famous beeswax sheets, you can do quite a few things with the next candles you make.

1. You can always cut the beeswax sheet in half to create shorter candles.

2. You can trim a sheet vertically, allowing you to make thinner candles.

3. You can also mix colors of beeswax in a single candle.

4. If you wish to engage in a few additional creative ideas, you can make tea lights using beeswax, and can use cookie cutters as well.

See? This one was extremely easy to make, and equally fun as well.

Get Creative

Of course, it takes a while for anyone to master these steps. However, the beauty is that once you have learned how to make these candles, you can then go on to explore your creative capabilities fully. Whether you do that as a hobby or for the business itself, you can explore the internet, check out various blogs and social posts, and gain new ideas. You can also learn more about potential opportunities, and by then you will be confident enough to create great masterpieces on your own.

Practice as much as you can. Right now, you have the time to do so. Once the business gets going, you may not be able to experiment or practice much. With that said, it is time to end this chapter and look forward to the new one.

Chapter 5:
Become a Real Competitor: Make Sure Your Candles Are High-Quality and Super Safe

Okay, this might sound a little too obvious, but bear with me on this one.

A lot of people I have helped over the years have shown tendencies of losing their quality, or overlooking simple safety issues. They start assuming that their customers will know what needs to be done, or that they will be too busy burning these candles away to notice the tiny flaws. The fact of the matter is that every customer who intends to buy candles keeps an eye out for even the tiniest details, and it is their right to do so. If we start overlooking these tiny aspects, we are not going to successfully establish our business at all.

This chapter dives into why both quality and safety are extremely important. It is a bit obvious that every business should focus on quality and the safety of both the workers and the consumers. Still, we will discover why they are so important, and how we can ensure that the products we are working upon are safe and of quality build.

Assumption is Fatal

This is one of the finest rules I have come across in life, and I have also gained significant experience to support the same as well. Never assume anything, especially when it comes to business.

You may compromise ever so slightly on quality, thinking the customers will not notice, but I assure you,

83

your customers will always keep an eye out. Granted that not all of them will be as eagle-eyed as others, but those who are can quickly bring your business to a screeching halt.

Then there is a problem with informing the consumers about all the safety issues with your products. If you were to assume they know how to use your candles or products safely, you would overlook the importance of a safety sticker and other information. You may not provide those, and that can often come back to haunt you. It only takes one accident, and that alone could be a solid reason for someone to sue your business for failing to provide the necessary information. What you will end up with is a significant blow to the business, and a massive compensation to pay.

Clearly, both these issues are essential, and both need to be catered to accordingly if you are to proceed to establish a successful business and one that continues to operate for ages to come.

Firstly, let us look at how we can tackle the primary function of a candle, and how we can ensure that we provide information to the customers.

Burning Safety

A candle is meant to be used eventually. They are not decorative pieces that remain on the countertop without ever being used. Eventually, someone will light the wick up, and that is where the candle must remain safe to be used. This part is something we can control during the production phase. By using the right materials and elements, we can ensure that the burning process is the safest for the end-users.

What isn't in our control is the environment the customer chooses to burn it in, or the way they decide to use the candle. There is a myriad of issues that need to be addressed, and the only thing we can do here is to provide the end-users with proper safety instructions and information.

Safety information isn't just a "keep away from children" sticker; it is a lot more than that. These little stickers provide important details to the end-users to ensure that the user knows how to use the product in the safest manner possible. Most of us have a habit of never even paying any attention to these instructions, but that is something we, the business owners, should never assume.

Regardless of the fact that the safety instructions could be overlooked or read clearly, we should always aim to provide them using appropriate labels and stickers. As candle makers, we must always assume the worst, and then move ahead with all the precautionary measures.

The first thing to do as a business is to assume that your customers do not know the proper method to burn candles. With that in mind, every candle you create must include a set of burning safety instructions. The National Candle Association and the Consumer Product Safety Commission views these as one of the most important aspects of any product. Overlook that, and you are already shooting yourself in the foot. This is mostly because both these institutes have a mechanism in place to ensure all candle makers follow some strict safety guidelines and provide information to the customers. Whether the customer decides to follow these instructions or not is an entirely separate issue.

"Exactly what kind of information should I provide to the customers?"

The candle burning instructions should always be clear and understandable. They should provide the end-users with critical performance information regarding the candle and should also inform customers about some core aspects that promote safety and ensure a good experience.

Start by providing information regarding the wick that your candle uses. You do not need to provide the name of the wick or the total length, as that would not classify as safety information. What you should, however, provide is a piece of information that lets the customers know how long the wick must be to burn safely. Here is a typical example that most candle makers use:

"The wick of the candle must be trimmed to one-fourth of an inch."

Then, there is the issue with debris being left on candles. Some debris may not be flammable, but once again, we must not assume anything. Let the customers know to ensure they "never leave any debris in the candle" to remain safe.

The time a candle takes to burn from top to bottom is also vital. This is to ensure that the candle users know how long the candle will take to burn. This information can, at times, make all the difference between a good experience and a horrific one. Generally speaking, a candle takes roughly around four hours to be used fully. Therefore, the instructions should say:

"Burn time associated with this candle is four hours."

Other important information to add includes:

- Never leave a burning candle unattended.

- The candle must always be used on a heat-resistant surface.
- Keep out of reach from children and pets.

Now comes the slightly easier part, which is to figure out where these safety instructions and reminders must be placed. The safety instructions must always be placed somewhere the customers can read easily. This is why most of the candles produced by candle makers have candle burning instructions right at the bottom of the candle itself. One reason is that it has a significant surface area, allowing candle makers to utilize the space with ease.

Tip: To encourage the consumers to read the candle burning instructions, use some unique features such as a sticker pointing towards the safety instructions, or something on the box. This ensures that the consumers are informed that the bottom of the candle holds something important.

Beyond Burning

Of course, the burning part is for the consumers to know, learn, and practice safely, but that does not mean that we, as individuals and as a business entity, are free to overlook these safety aspects. We, too, have some safety issues that we must also consider.

While we are more concerned with the production of the candles, there are quite a few things that can still go wrong should we not follow some rules and abide by some safety protocols. Since we are dealing with a product that is used with fire, we should always ensure that the material and supplies we use are safe to be used around fires.

I have come across quite a few tragic stories about candle makers ending up with a massive blaze ruining almost everything and anything that came in its grip. This can happen to the best of us at times, which is why the following are some great safety tips to keep in consideration when working with and producing candles.

1. You should always know the size of the wick that needs to be used. It should always be the proper size. Have it too long, and you risk setting things on fire nearby, or at least damaging the candle from the outside. This must be made sure for each candle you create.

2. Many containers on the market can be used to hold candles, and you might even be tempted to try something different. However, know that not all containers are approved to withstand the temperatures of a candle fire. They may burst, crack, and cause harm to others nearby. Always choose to use containers that are specifically approved to be used for candle making.

3. Get to know your waxes and fragrances better. Once again, there are many which are available in the market, but not all are able to work well with each other. Get a fragrance that has alcohol in it, and you risk setting the entire candle on fire, or worse.

4. Always ensure that you do not include anything flammable near the burning area. It may seem like a no-brainer, but I have heard of people ending up doing that. Your safety, and the safety of those who may be working with you, is of importance.

5. Learn how your candle performs in various scenarios and situations. It helps teach you where your candles perform the best, and where they may become a bit of a hazard. You can always include such findings in the candle burning instructions.

With that said, let us look at how we can maintain high quality for our products. It goes without saying that higher quality will always attract more customers, but there are other things which can get in the way, and may cause things to go a bit sideways.

Maintaining Quality

This may seem a bit easy, and quite a lot of readers may think that they can maintain the quality by ensuring that they continue to buy quality products. You wouldn't be completely wrong, but there are other challenges besides the purchasing of material and supplies that can easily cause you to lose track of quality.

Here are a few things which should help make things a bit easier and allow you to maintain control of the quality of your products. You can note these down separately and use the information as a quick reminder of what you need to do when things get going.

1. Never take more orders than you can manage. Making money is a very, very interesting part of any business. There is no denying that once the money starts to roll in, you will want more of it to come your way. That is perfectly fine, but do not let yourself be caught up in the rat race just yet. Right now, you are most likely the only person operating your business with some help, if any, from your friend, family member, or spouse. This means that you can only manage a

set number of orders per day or per week. Find out your optimal production capacity and keep track of the incoming orders. The second the order number crosses your threshold, pause all incoming orders, or line them up for the next week. Controlling your workflow is essential, and it is equally important that you only take on what you can manage. Only then can you maintain your quality and not rush through things, which is generally when things go wrong.

2. Write down the recipes, the measurements, and the instructions clearly. Keep notes about what you do, what you add, the duration of the process, the temperatures, humidity levels, and everything you can gather. You will need all the information you can get to continue creating great candles. There will come a time when you may go on exploring new ideas, and that is when keeping notes will greatly help you out.

3. Keep an eye out for all the variables around you that you can control. The more you control these variables, the better you can focus on retaining a good quality of your products.

4. It is vital that you inquire with your supplier regarding the materials and supplies you purchase from them. It is a very common thing to find that a supplier will always try and change their source for acquiring these materials and supplies, to suit their finances and budget better. While this may be good for their business, it is definitely not good for us candle makers. You should always check to see if they continue to provide you with supplies and other essentials from the same source. This ensures uniformity

of your products, and hence takes away any chances of quality depreciation.

5. When it comes to additives, they can be a bit tricky to measure. This is why I mentioned earlier in the book that you will require things like pipettes or measuring jars. You will need to ensure that you always use the optimum measurements when adding additives to the mix. Do not take this lightly, as this can significantly change the outcome of the product.

You can create a checklist of items to ensure that each step you do is completed as per your guidelines. This further helps you know that the products you create are of the same quality as always.

When customers buy your products and they receive the same quality every time, they will automatically trust you as their preferred candle maker. Winning the trust of the consumers is the ultimate goal of any business in existence. It is through their trust that we get more sales, referrals, and more.

With that said, there is but one issue that still needs to be addressed. We discussed candle burning instructions, but what about the burn time? How on earth do we measure that? Let us look into that before moving on to the next chapter.

Establishing Candle Burning Time

You may be creating an array of candle types and designs. With each candle that you make, you should always know what the maximum burning time for the candle is supposed to be. This is an important piece of research on your end and an essential bit of consumer information that must be included in the candle burning instructions.

The burn time should always match with the one printed on the label. Besides, establishing the burning time allows you to know whether your product is of the quality you expect it to be or otherwise. It can also serve as a terrific marketing tool as well.

One primary reason to know your candle's burn time is to answer queries that the consumers may have easily. Take it from a person who has dealt with such queries for years. Consumers often ask, "which one of your candles offers the maximum burning time?" If I had no idea, I might not have been able to answer confidently, and that would have created a negative impression on the potential customer. By knowing your data and the facts, you will always be confident about your product and the information related to it.

This process is a little easy because you already have a general benchmark to compare your time with. There is no strict rule nor any regulation that determines how long a candle should burn. It is generally expected that most candles will have a burn time of around four hours before blowing out.

After the candle blows out, wait for a minimum of an hour and then relight the candle. You must follow this procedure until the entire candle is consumed. During the process, note down the time. By the end, you should have an average time with you. Using that average time, you can compare with the benchmark to learn how well or otherwise your candle performs.

Other essential information which you also need to note includes:

- The extent of smoke
- Any mushrooming that may occur
- Any other key characteristics

By using the method above, you will also gain valuable information regarding the wick size you are using. If your wick size is of the right length and quality, you should notice different and more promising results.

Here are some additional tips to further help you know more about the wick you are using:

- After the burn cycle is completed, if you find some wax on the sides of the candle's container, this should indicate that the wick you are using is too small. If you see such results, consider increasing the length of the wick you are using.

- In case you burn through all the wax and you witness excessive soot and smoking, this means you are using a much longer wick than necessary. Consider trimming it down.

- There may be cases where your candle's wick may "drown out" in the middle of a burning cycle. If so, your wick was a little too small.

- If your new candle is burning faster as compared to the other ones you may have recorded times for, this would suggest that your wick was far too large.

Selecting the right type of wick is perhaps one of the most important components in ensuring a high-quality product. It may take a bit of time, especially if you are experimenting with newer designs and types, but once you are confident and your data supports your optimism, bring those wicks into production.

Now it is time to look forward to our next chapter. This is where we will learn how to narrow down our niche, which will further help you ensure your success as a business.

Chapter 6:
Time to Get Serious: Narrow Down Your Niche

Earlier in the book, we discovered that despite being a niche market, the market for candles is still significant in size and number. There are millions of consumers just within the USA, let alone the world. Sure enough, we cannot expect to win the entire market overnight. Neither do we have the capital, the marketing budget, or the production capacity to mass-produce candles at such a massive scale. Something must be done to ensure that we can first acquire the right kind of customers, control the orders, and serve them accordingly. Fortunately, just by narrowing down your niche, you can do most of the above right away.

When it comes to our niche, it isn't just 'candle making.' There are a lot of variables which further help us define the kind of niche we are targeting. Even changing the type of candles you make can alter the niche you work for. For example, someone who prefers to create jewelry candles would never work on rolled or dipped candles. Their target market would also be more interested in buying jewelry candles and would not prefer to purchase any other type of candles.

It is indeed tricky, but narrowing down your niche can help you save quite a lot of hassle, worry, expense, and a lot more. This chapter will look into how we can narrow down our niche, and how that will further help us narrow down the niche market we are trying to target.

It's All About Niche

Let us start with a small fact. Currently, there are around 361 candle manufacturing companies in existence within the US alone (Walker, n.d.). I may not seem like much to you, and to some extent, you aren't wrong.

Candle users are millions in numbers. In fact, every seven out of 10 households use candles (Candle Science, n.d.). That is a significant number, and it only goes on to encourage us, candle makers, knowing that our chances of selling candles are rather high.

For you to be in a comfortable position, it is vital that you know what kind of products, or candles, you aim to produce and sell. It is also important that you target the market that this niche would be most appropriate in. Ending up with your chosen niche in the wrong market would result in virtually no sales at all, leading to a complete loss and a possible closure of the business.

This part takes a bit of a trial and error approach, but you can always skip past that by studying your competitors closely. There are many ways you can find your niche market easily, and one of them is through today's ultimate marketing tool: social media.

Using Facebook, Instagram, and some other platforms, you can filter through the kinds of people who may be explicitly interested in the type of candles you are trying to produce and sell. You do not have to start a paid promotion campaign necessarily, but these tools should provide you with a rough estimate of how large your niche market is, as well as other important information such as their geographic location, gender, age, other related interests, and so on. You can use that data to improve your marketing strategy further.

An excellent way to ensure that your product attracts attention is to have a good business plan. To get you started, here are some great tips that can help you achieve a flying start. Learn these, and then apply the same to your own business. Once again, I do not imply that the results will start pouring in right away. It takes a bit of time, but rest assured, the results will come.

1. Start with a great name - Naming your product is the most important aspect of them all. It is the name that goes on to create impressions, and it is the name that goes on to serve as the identity of the company. There are hundreds and thousands of name ideas you can find on the internet, and that means finding one should not be hard at all. However, be sure that the name is:

   a. Quirky

   b. Easy to remember

   c. Easy to spell

   d. Catchy

   e. Unique

2. While the name of a product is certainly something that attracts attention, another thing that continues to prove helpful is the packaging itself. Even top-quality products can go unnoticed if appropriate packaging is not considered. Your packaging tells a lot about the kind of business you are. This is why you will always find the best products in the finest packaging material and design. When companies use sub-par or just mediocre packaging, people simply walk past them.

3. If your candles use fragrances or you intend to have a lineup of scented candles, try not to follow your competitors. To gain a competitive

advantage, you will need to come up with a unique fragrance, something that has not been used before, and has the charm and scent to attract those passing by. You cannot imagine how easily you can win a customer just by providing a blend of unique and refreshing elements to create a scent that lasts.

4. If you mention your support for charitable causes, you will stand out from your competition with ease. It will allow other consumers and potential customers to know that you donate a part of your profits to support a specified charity organization or institute. Taking part in a charitable cause is rewarding in so many different ways.

Your goal, obviously, is to sell as many candles as possible. However, just because you need to sell them does not mean that they should be ordinary. You should sell unique and distinctive candles that consumers simply cannot find anywhere else. As long as you maintain your quality, your customers will keep on coming back.

The Process Itself

You might be thinking about how exactly you can narrow down your niche to make things a little easier for yourself and be able to do good business. Well, the wait is over, as I will take you through the process. Take notes where needed, as this information will greatly help you in figuring out what your niche may be. If you feel lost, you can always refer back to these notes for a quick reminder.

The first thing is to be sure about whether you intend to set up your business online or in a brick and mortar

98

store. Both have their advantages and disadvantages. You must get this sorted out first.

Once you have that out of the way, it is time to start with the process of narrowing down your niche. Right away, the first thing is to evaluate your skills and passion. That is a bit of an obvious one, or so one would think.

"What do you mean, 'evaluate?' I know I am a candle maker."

True, but that is not what I meant. You are indeed a candle maker, but what type of candles do you make? Are you choosing to create a candle or follow a niche just because you find it interesting? If so, stop.

You must always pursue a niche that is sustainable. It should be something that will stretch on for a long duration. It should also be something that you can see yourself doing passionately for the next five years or longer. The field you target should be one in which you have special skills and/or experience. This is where you may use the feedback you gathered earlier from your family members, neighbors, and friends.

If you have some special training in specific products or niches, it would be a good idea to begin with that. The sweet spot is targeting an area where you have certain skills or experience, and that you are passionate about. Since the work can get repetitive, your passion can ensure that you never feel bored and that your morale is always high.

The next step is to find out if the type of niche you are targeting has any demand within the market. Of course, targeting one that has no demand would be futile. You would not be able to sell anything, and no one who came across your products would be interested in choosing them. This is why it is very important to choose a niche that has a market. Once you have decided on a niche, you can look around to see if there are competitors and learn how well they are doing. A higher number of sales suggests a higher demand.

While we have learned how to find more about niche markets through the use of social media, there is yet another good way to gain more information. You can use a tool called Google Keyword Planner. This is one of the easiest methods, and one of the most accurate as well, to find out how in-demand a specific keyword is. It is generally used for something called Search Engine Optimization (SEO), which helps blogs and websites to retain a higher rank and gather organic traffic.

Using the Google Keyword Planner, you can find out just how much a certain keyword is searched for and get a significant idea of how large the market for a particular niche is. If you are aiming to create votive candles, use the keyword planner and search for keywords such as votive candles, fancy candles, candlemaker near me, best candles 2021, and any other keywords you can recall. Gather the information, and soon you should have a fair idea of how large or otherwise your targeted niche market is.

Here are some additional tips for using Google Keyword Planner:

- 1K-10K range - Under the search volume, you will come across various numbers and ranges. For the safest results, stick to the ones between this range. Anything less than this would mean that there is virtually no market, and anything higher would indicate that the market is already saturated.

- Low-Medium Competition - For the competition, keep it low-medium in size to ensure you do not end up facing stiff competition right in the beginning.

- Higher suggested bids - This one may be a bit technical, but you should stick to this. If I start teaching you what this does, I would also need to inform you about AdWords, AdSense, ads, and so much more, and that would deviate us from the topic.

The next step after the above is to narrow down the niche further using all the information you have collected so far. Now, find out whether your niche falls under a specific category. Since we are talking about candles, they can be either all-natural or synthetic. Then, go on to further narrow your product down to its unique characteristics. If your candles have scents, extended burning times, or creative designs, use those to filter out your niche further.

Remember, if your candles can be described using a general term such as containers or votives, your candles are lacking an identity of their own. If you use fragrances, consider placing your products under the niche "aromatic all-natural candles," as this would suit them better and would go on to attract the appropriate audience.

Knowing your competition is your next step after narrowing down your niche. While going through the keyword search and gathering the facts and figures is undoubtedly an important aspect, you must also know what the competition is like.

First of all, google the same keywords you searched for earlier on, and use some of the suggested ones as well. You will be able to see many websites ranking right at the top. If there are a lot of sites ranking at the top, or the search result pours in a vast number of relevant websites, that would suggest that the niche you are targeting is oversaturated.

On the off chance that you are unable to see any relevant sites listed, that would suggest that no one searches for such keywords, and that there is absolutely no demand for this niche. It is also possible that this niche simply does not exist. In either case, this is a risky niche to target. There are certainly a lot of opportunities, but the converse can be equally dire.

Finally, you may come across some websites which are ranked but are clearly not of high quality, nor do they provide promising results. That is the kind of setting ideal for you to enter. This would mean that you do not have to put in extra effort to create websites or pages with extensive budgets. Even the simplest would do nicely. This is the type of market that is promising and holds significant opportunities for you. This would imply that the niche you have chosen is currently in its ideal state for a startup.

Now that the niche is defined and the market is observed, it is time to test your niche. A good way would be to use surveys to start gathering data. Through surveys, you can find out the potential demand, customer sentiments, and their ideas about the perfect candle, plus a lot more valuable information.

Another way would be to create websites and start driving traffic to your landing page by using AdWords or other advertising platforms. You will learn how your products are performing and how much potential interest they are garnering. This, combined with the surveys, should provide you with a good idea of how your niche would perform. Keeping the results in consideration, you can then go on to take the appropriate actions.

Defining Your Products

Candlemakers often go on to sell additional products. In your case, know what products you would be selling. These could be the candles themselves, as well as containers, specialized/personalized candle holders, fragrances, or anything else for that matter. Whatever you intend to sell, you must define it clearly.

As a business entity, you cannot just go on saying that you sell candles. Are they home-made? Are they all-natural? Do they come with fragrances? What types are they? What kind of burning time do they provide? Everything must be defined explicitly for your business and for the potential customer to know.

Other aspects to consider and work on include:

- The type of products with fragrances would you be selling
- The selling prices for these products
- Where you will be purchasing your supplies from
- Cost of supplies
- Production cost

By working on these aspects and gathering all the relevant information, you will go on to better understand your products and services. You will need to know all you can about your products and business, and that will undoubtedly come into play when you are trying to acquire the necessary permits and approvals from the relative authorities. You will need to provide as much information as possible and satisfy the requirements from each of these institutions before they provide you with the necessary permits to operate freely.

Speaking about permits, there are laws all of us candle makers have to abide by. In the next chapter, we will look into what these are and how we can ensure we abide by them. We will also be looking into how packaging plays a part in the overall customer experience, and any specific legal requirements we should know about.

Chapter 7:
Protecting Yourself and Your Product: Labeling, Packaging, and Laws

When customers buy our candles, the first thing that they get to see is the packaging. This means, dare I say, the packaging is where the customer is won or lost. Behind every good product goes hours and hours of thoughts, trial and error, and numerous designs before a finalized design and packaging material is decided.

Our products are packed not because they look better that way, but because we need to ensure they are safe from harm and that the customer gets to use them in the finest condition possible. The only way to do so is to pack your products nicely, but there are hundreds of variables that come into play. The type of packaging, any particular laws which govern the use of such products and packages, and anything else that may have an impact on the product itself must be kept into consideration.

There are quite a few legal requirements in place to ensure all candle makers continue to operate safely, and that these laws protect both the producers and consumers. While we will be discussing some of these laws, all of which apply to the US, it is always a good idea to inquire about your local laws if you reside in a different country.

Product-Related Information

We have learned almost everything we can about the candle making process. We have also learned so much about how we can find our niche and learn how to target some of the desired market, if not all of it. The next step is to review your product as a whole, and that includes the packaging it comes in.

Of course, you cannot expect all your products to have the same packaging. They may use the same materials, but if you are offering a range of products, you will need to ensure that each product type has its very own packaging. This further gives your product an identity, and helps consumers to identify your product from a mile away.

The packaging is important, but what is equally important is the use of labels. Previously, we looked into using labels that provide consumers with candle burning instructions. It isn't recommended that you only use a single label, or one that specifically talks about burning characteristics. You can do a lot more with labels.

The labels are your one and perhaps only shot at communicating directly with the consumers or end-users. Whether you aim to distribute your candles to retailers or sell them directly to end-users, your label will be the only thing that communicates to the consumers what needs to be done, or what kind of safety measures they should take. You will not be able to tell every single consumer everything, and if you try to do so you will bring the entire operation to a halt. To save time, we use labels.

"So, what do I include in a label?"

I am glad you asked that question. Besides the entire burning quality aspect we learned about earlier, we can enter some information about:

- Unique features
- Benefits

- Safety instructions
- Information regarding scents or size of wick
- Any/all UPC codes
- Contact information
- Website
- Any unique selling point (USP) which you may wish to include

While everything seems to be in order, there is one thing that I must go on to explain, and that is the UPC code.

Some products are sold throughout the world, and you may have come across the fact that these products come with their own unique barcodes. These are seemingly universal, meaning that they do not change throughout the world. These codes follow specific laws that make them accepted globally. They serve as the product identifiers. I know this may sound intimidating and slightly deviated from the topic as well, but every candle maker needs to learn about these.

If you are to sell your products locally, you do not need to worry about getting yourself a UPC code. These are only used when you intend to expand your reach and start selling your products globally.

Within the US, the product identifier is the UPC number (GTIN-12). This UPC number consists of two key components. The first is the company prefix, and the second is the product number. Within the US, GS1 is the local US company that manages the entire database of company prefixes. In other words, the company prefix is licensed by your local GS1 office. The GS1 is also responsible for the "establishment and implementation of global commerce standards for markings and communication." (Bar Code Graphics Inc., n.d.).

To summarize, you will need the UPC code if you wish to sell your products globally. You can skip this if you are only trying to sell within the local crafts and hobby stores.

"I guess it wouldn't hurt to register. Who knows? I might find more customers globally."

Well, in that case, let me talk you through how you can get a barcode for your product.

1. You will need to apply for a GS1 company prefix.

2. Next, you will need to assign a unique product number.

3. Figure out how you would like your product to display the barcode.

4. Order your UPC barcodes.

You can always visit the GS1 website, and you can get in touch with them in case you run into any issues, or you need additional help.

The Box that Matters

With the technicalities out of the way, it is time to start focusing a little on the packaging, or the box, that we will be using with our product. This is where the impression of a customer is won or lost. You may have the most delicate candle in the business, but if you pack it in a shabby looking package, virtually everyone will walk right past it.

Boxes can be simple. As long as your package is a part of your product, it will do well. What do I mean by "part of your product," I hear you say? That is simple. The box should look like it belongs to the product. If you start packing your candles in a regular box, it might give a negative impression. The box should at least include the brand name, information about the type of candle it holds, and a USP.

To make things even more elegant, include your contact information and use some of the space to speak to your market, using the USPs effectively. You should always keep in mind that the unboxing is a significant part of the customer's experience. In fact, these days, YouTube is brimming with content where customers post videos about the unboxing experience. If you ruin that moment for the customer, it will not bode well for the future of the company.

If you wish to make things a little more interesting, you can always google some designers and hire them to work on your packaging. Investing a little money and coming up with elegant designs can often go a long way.

The boxes themselves can be bought from your preferred wholesaler. Buying them in bulk and at a wholesale rate can save you a chunk of money. With that sorted, all that remains now is to acquaint yourself with a few laws within the USA that every candlemaker must follow.

We already know that the NCA has played a significant role in ensuring the entire industry continues to follow regulations and that the candle makers exercise safety and caution for themselves, their workers, and the end-users. ASTM International develops these regulations. If you are someone who is wanting to sell within the United States, I urge you to visit ASTM's website and check out all the legal requirements there.

It is worth a look, and it will provide you with a significant idea of what you need to do to ensure you and your products continue to satisfy the legalities involved. Overlooking these may create legal opportunities for your rivals to use against you. It is relatively common that when a business starts flying, other competitors may resort to legal loopholes and exploit the same to gain an advantage, even if that means the worst for some other company.

The ASTM website will provide you with all the relevant information you need. It is also the perfect place to learn all about the laws that apply to all the candle makers within the US. It is a good idea to keep checking this website once or twice every quarter of the year, just to ensure that you are up-to-date with the laws. Any amendments or additions will be reflected here. If you spot one, you can take the necessary steps to ensure you comply with the laws.

The boxes you will go on to use must contain information that is truthful in nature, clear, and free of any bias. The labels you use, either on the candles or the boxes, must be placed neatly, especially on the product itself. This is to ensure that they do not pose a fire risk, which is easily the case if you end up pasting the labels in the wrong position.

Most of the candle types should pose little to no problem when packing them in boxes. When it comes to votive and container candles, you may need to use additional cushioning and a fragile label to ensure that they are packed correctly and the handler handles them carefully. With that done, all that remains is for these candles to be shipped, transported, and delivered to the destination. The business is all set to go, and with that, it is time now to move forward to the next chapter. Pay attention to this one, because so far we have assumed that our business is working. No one ever mentioned anything about getting the business off the ground, right? That is exactly what we will be discussing next.

Chapter 8:
Business Basics: Getting Your Candle Making Business Off the Ground

The basic idea behind any business is universal: to sell something in exchange for money. With that said, however, there are a million other factors that come into play, and each one of these variables changes the way a business operates. This also means that the things which affect the growth or downfall of business also continue to change, as per these factors.

Luckily for us at least, our business involves making candles and selling them. There is no rocket science involved here, and neither do we need to pursue a master's degree in order to ensure success. Anyone can make this business into a success, as long as they understand the basics involved behind operating a business and ensuring its success.

This chapter, therefore, will teach you what these business basics are, how they affect your business, and what you need to do in order to get your business off the ground.

Business 101

Passion alone cannot take you places. It can certainly introduce you to a wealth of knowledge, possibilities, and ideas, but how you use that knowledge and what you do with these ideas has nothing to do with passion. What you need is a solid plan, and for that you must know the basics of the business you intend to set up.

The number one rule behind any successful business is to spend time. I am not talking about giving it a couple of hours a day. You will need to invest as much time as possible. In short, the more time you invest in your business, the better the outcome will be. Of course, the time you will put in must be productive and meaningful. Merely sitting around doing nothing would serve you no purpose. If a person cannot commit to this, it is perhaps time to drop the idea and explore something else that may not require effort and time.

Any business, even Amazon and Facebook, requires its owners and workers to continue investing time. Without their contribution into the business, the world would have never known these names. Once you have made up your mind and promised yourself that you will put in the necessary time, it is time to move ahead.

The first step is jotting down a great business plan. The good news is that the internet is full of information. You can browse multiple websites to gain some inspiration for your business plan. A business plan, in essence, is a plan of action. It defines what you will need to do, how your business will start things off, and what goals it will go on to pursue. Writing a business plan, especially today, is neither tough nor fussy at all.

A business plan involves six vital components. These six components will determine whether you have a workable business plan in place, or if it needs any improvement. You can always refine your idea if you feel something is off, but you will always need to ensure that all six components are covered. Your business plan is incomplete if you miss out on any of these.

Executive Summary

The Executive Summary is a summarized overview of what your business is all about and what your plans are.

This is the first component of any business plan. It is also to be noted that a lot of people prefer to write it last, to ensure that they can cover everything mentioned in the plan.

Opportunity

This section is where things start to take shape. The opportunity segment answers three vital questions:

1. What are you selling?

2. How are you solving a market need or problem?

3. Who is your competition and target market?

Execution

As the name suggests, this section is where you will answer one important question that mostly relates to how you intend to execute your plans. This question is:

- How do you intend to utilize the opportunity and make it into a profitable business?

Company Summary

This is also known as the management summary. Apart from the executive summary, this summary provides investors with yet another reason why they should go on to invest in your business. Investors always keep an eye out for great teams behind equally great ideas, and they get to know all about the team in this part of the business plan.

In this section, you will describe the kind of people you wish to hire, and the ones who are already a part of your business. You can also provide information regarding the legal structure, history, and location of your business (in case you are already operating).

Financial Plans

Of course, without the financial plan, a business plan is never complete. In this segment of the plan, you will provide sales forecasts, cash flow statements, your profits and losses (also known as income statements), and the balance sheets as well.

Appendix

This is the final segment of the business plan. This is where you will include product images, any additional information, or key features that you wish investors to go through.

Combine all of these, and you end up with a solid business plan. You can use these plans to pitch proposals to potential investors and others who may be interested in working alongside you.

It is certainly a bit intimidating for someone who may have never created a business plan before, but I assure you, you will need this to test out your idea. The results will only be informative and encouraging for those who do not mind learning from their mistakes. Starting a business without a business plan is both risky and a bit silly. By having a business plan, you allow yourself to:

- Test your ideas
- Provide your business with the best possible chances of succeeding
- Help secure funding
- Attract investors
- Make planning a lot more manageable and effective

Besides having a marketing plan, you will also need to come up with a business name. Your business name must be easy to read and understandable, and it should be unique, as it will go on to serve as your business identity. The business name should reflect the kind of business you are into. You will need to check at the Secretary of State's website and see if the name of your choice is available. You would be surprised to know just how quickly good names get registered, making the entire naming exercise a lot harder.

You can also run a search on Google and try to find any trademarks associated with the name you are using. There are hundreds of thousands of ways a name can be used, and checking each of these out yourself can be a bit cumbersome. This is why our dear friend Google is something we can rely upon. Once you are sure that the name you have chosen is not used anywhere, you can register your business using said name.

It is also a good idea to immediately reserve yourself an appropriate domain name for your website. You can also create other social media accounts, pages, and communities to ensure that the name is not used by someone other than you.

Once you have the names reserved, it is time to start thinking of the type of business entity you intend to own. Are you more interested in being a sole-proprietor, or do you wish to have a partnership? Do you intend to expand further and take full advantage of being a limited liability company? These are the type of questions you should be able to answer on your own. Think it through and take your time. If you have a partner or two in mind, it is best to discuss this now so that you can plan accordingly.

If you aren't too sure, you can always consult a business attorney. Alternatively, you can also speak to a tax expert to learn which is better for you. Once this is sorted, you will then need to register your company with the federal and state agencies.

Get all the licenses and permits you require to operate independently and confidently. Operating without acquiring these licenses is illegal, and can land you in a world of trouble. If you need to wait a little longer, do so, but ensure you always get your papers in order. It is to be noted that laws or license requirements may vary from locality to locality. Consult the official SBA website to find out what you will need to do in order to acquire a license and a permit.

You will also need insurance, in case anything goes wrong. I would recommend that you start with small business insurance. This is ideal if you intend to have a business that is only operated by you. You can always upgrade the type of insurance you have, which will come in handy if you decide to expand and hire more people.

Additional Things to Remember

Use the business plan to define your products further. You will need to consider the following factors when determining the kind of products you have:

- The type of product you intend to sell

- What you intend to charge for the product

When it comes to setting a price for the product, you will need to focus on your total cost of production and the target market you are working with. How do you know your total cost? Simple!

- **Variable Cost** - These are expenses that can vary, depending on how many candles you make.

117

- **Fixed Cost** - These are expenses that remain constant no matter how many candles you make.

- **Total Cost** - Simply add these two together, and you end up with the total cost.

Now that you have your cost figured out, it is time to set the price accordingly. A traditional method would call for a price that is two times the cost. This is typically true in the case that you intend to be a wholesaler. For retail prices, it should be three times the cost.

Alternatively, you can always aim to set profit margins. Typically, a good margin is 25% to 50% at most, based on your cost. This margin is good for new businesses that are entering the market. In your case, if you are new, you will need to rely on these margins and later change the prices accordingly, once the business is established.

I know you might be wondering how you can know if the price is right. Obviously, you need some kind of benchmark to compare your prices with. This is why I decided to do a bit of research on my own, and provide you with some numbers to consider. Below are average prices of a 5.8oz candle:

- Mass market - $5 to $8
- Mid-market - $9 to $14
- High-end market - $15 to $22

Depending on your niche, you will fall in one of these three categories. You can now compare your prices easily and know whether your prices are attractive or otherwise.

You will also need to keep in consideration the source of your supplies, and the cost. You can always search around to see if you can get a better deal, but try not to opt for suppliers that are far away, or cannot assure you timely and regular deliveries.

You can always opt for a bit of extra funding for your business. Some additional financial assistance can certainly help you to pay for the suppliers and any liabilities you may have. You can use various channels to accumulate funds or gain access to financial benefits and assistance. These include, but are not limited to:

- **Business lines of credit** - A line of credit that provides a set amount of money. It can be withdrawn when needed.

- **Business credit cards** - These are a better option as opposed to loans. With zero percent APR, you theoretically have an interest-free way to purchase things at the start of your business.

- **Equipment financing** - This is specific to candle makers who are going to produce candles on a much larger scale.

- **Startup funding** - This caters to all the initial expenses and gets you started.

Finally, you will need to keep a strict eye on your inventory. This is where a lot of businesses falter and often find themselves stuck.

Managing your inventory effectively will require you to know how much stock you have at any given time. You should also know how much stock you will be consuming a day and what you will have by the end of the day, the week, and so on. You can write these numbers down or hire a programmer to create a program and digitalize all the information. Alternatively, you can always use the inventory management systems available online on platforms like Etsy, Shopify, Amazon, and much more. You will need to put in the initial efforts, but once done, every time you sell something, the inventory will reflect the change accordingly.

You should also know your reorder point. This is essentially a number of stocks which indicate that you will need to reorder something from your supplier before you run out. You can find more about inventory management online, and you can even hire freelancers to do a program for you for better inventory management.

Next, we will be looking into how you can market your candles for better sales and success. This will be short, but it is every bit as important as any other chapter.

Chapter 9:
Making Your Business
a Success: How to Market Your
Candles

Having learned all this so far is great, but you always need to know how to market your candles. The customers, after all, will never go out to find who you are. You need to use a few of your marketing tools and skills to create desire and want for your products.

Your products should contain some form of appeal that attracts customers to carry out the action and buy your products. You have hundreds of thousands of ways to do so. This is the power of marketing. Even something as small as a sentence can make all the difference, and can flood in orders beyond your capacity.

In this chapter, we will look into some essentials you should know to market your candles better. This chapter will be brief, but that is to ensure that we do not indulge in any unnecessary or complicated issues at this point.

Marketing 101

Earlier, we learned a bit about the basics of business. In this section, we will learn a little about marketing. We will not be going too far into the details, and that is because most people already know what marketing is. Instead, we will be discussing a few technicalities which could certainly help you market your products a little better. For that, we will be looking to create a marketing plan.

Define Marketing Goals

Every marketing campaign has a goal that it must achieve. Similarly, you too, will need to know what your marketing goals are. You should know what you aim to accomplish through this marketing campaign. You will also need to understand how a marketing campaign will go on to contribute to your overall business goals.

You can begin by highlighting your USPs. Of course, this is where you will highlight the salient features or the unique aspects of your product, without lying or being biased.

Be specific about your marketing goals. Claiming that you wish to attract a lot of new customers is both vague and wrong. Instead, use a realistic number that you can go on to achieve through the marketing campaign. Your marketing campaign goals can be to:

- Generate new leads

- Generate website traffic

- Increase engagement rates on your Facebook, Twitter or other social media profiles and pages

- Conversion to sales

Social media plays a vital part in business these days, and that has more to do with the fact that it is free to use for everyone. Yes, there are some features which would require you to pay some amount of money, but most of the marketing can be done for free.

While you continue to market your products online on blogs, social media platforms, and websites, do not forget to sell your products physically as well. Through physical interaction with customers, you get real feedback. You also get a chance to discover new opportunities of being a wholesaler.

If you can get your customers to fill out forms, you may be able to gather data, especially the email addresses of customers. You can use those to push out email newsletters. You can populate the list, and you can continue to gain more attention.

Whether online or otherwise, you will need to market yourself as much as your product. You will do so by ensuring you provide as much information and act as knowledgeable as possible. You may often attract customers who may be drawn by the confidence you reflect in your product. Give out your business cards to as many people as possible. Ensure that your business card includes contact information and social media links. This will also go on to generate more traffic and potential sales as well.

Web Presence

Apart from all of the above, you will also need to have a fully functioning website. This will provide you with the web presence you need to capitalize on the traffic that exists on the internet. You can cash in on this endless traffic by using blog posts, and through newsletters. You can also provide a photo gallery of products that you produce. You should ensure consistency in posting relevant news and updates to ensure that your customers know exactly what your business is doing.

A large chunk of your orders will be placed by women, which is why it is important to keep this in mind when creating your marketing plan, online or otherwise. You will need to ensure that you cater to this market segment and provide them with a solid reason to buy your products. Let them know how your product is different, and how it can offer them a better experience.

Your marketing strategy must also include the kind of one-liner you will use to define your product. If you are dealing with several products, come up with catchy and creative names. If your candles use fragrances, think of combining the fragrance name with the candle, such as 'citrus fizz' or anything else that is creative. Creative names tend to attract more attention than "scented candles."

This information should serve you well enough to ensure your marketing campaign gets a jump-start. Finally, it is time for you to know how you can maintain your momentum once it starts building. The last chapter looks into how you can do just that and turn your candles into profits.

Chapter 10:
On a Roll: How to Keep Your Business Running Smoothly and Turn Your Candles into Profits

Every business that starts must eventually lead somewhere. The trouble is that quite a few grow impatient, and this impatience can lead to a premature downfall of the company.

As a business owner, it is up to you to give your business some time for it to grow and become successful. Do not expect your business to be a story-book perfect business that grows instantly overnight.

This chapter will look into what you will need to do to ensure your business continues to live on and remain profitable throughout.

Pay Attention

Your business is just like a child. Just as any child needs upbringing, love, care, and time, your business too will need all of that. You will need to pay as much attention to your business as you can just to make sure it works, let alone is profitable or otherwise. You, as the business owner, cannot go on to neglect, overlook, or underestimate any aspect of the business. Every bit is as important as any other one.

However, it is understandable that you might find yourself feeling overwhelmed, or just not the right fit for a specific aspect of the business. You can hire help for such tasks. Alternatively, you can outsource the business itself.

Outsourcing your business will eventually start reaping your profits for you. This move can be very beneficial and would be a good investment. However, remember that you will need to pay attention to management at the start before you can start reaping the profits.

You can also outsource specific business aspects such as sales, chat support, and so on. This would mean that while you pay attention to certain aspects of the business, someone else who is better equipped and qualified will handle a part that isn't exactly your forte.

Keep an eye on your progress. Check everything and, if needed, re-evaluate your business where and when necessary. You can always consider changing prices, changing the kind of supplies you use, introducing a new version of a candle, or even more. An effective business plan continually evolves with time, and adapts to changes as they come.

Your goals must be divided into small and achievable segments. Your initial goal will be to recover the cost of production. Once done, your ultimate goal will be to start making profits. Achieving the break-even point (the point where you are no longer at a loss but not yet making profits), will take some time, which is why you will need to be determined, patient, and focused.

Once you achieve the break-even point, you can continue to bring a few changes to grow your business further. These moves could include things such as:

- Adding new types of candles to the existing range
- Diversifying your product range, such as by adding lamps or fragrances
- Consider offering physical or online classes

- Consider franchising - If the demand has grown, and your business finds that it can do even better at another location, it is the ideal thing to do.

Franchising would require you to know the laws that apply to your business, and to the location where you are aiming to franchise your business. You will also need to consider the following with the second party (franchisee):

- Royalty and franchise fee
- Terms of franchise agreement
- Size of territory you will award your franchise
- The geographic area you intend to offer franchise in
- Type and length of the training program
- Whether said franchise should buy products from your company
- How you intend to market the franchise
- Business experience and net worth franchisees need

You can hire a lawyer to help you sort these out and ensure that you operate within the boundaries of the law.

Final Suggestions

Use recent market research data to know the current trends, and improve your business by adapting to the trends and changes. The quicker you do so, the better you will compete against the competition.

You will also need to work on your branding, and for that, you can rely on surveys and feedback. This will allow you to know whether your brand is familiar to the masses. If not, you can then target your branding and take the necessary actions to promote your brand's name and image within the market.

You will also need to understand what your customers want and need. Using that data, you can then go on to design and create candles that better suit their needs.

Your marketing campaign must be effective, which is why you must keep an eye on how effective your marketing plans are. If they are providing you with satisfactory results, all is good, but where you see it faltering, consider reviewing your marketing plans.

Using the new market research data, you can often come across new opportunities. If you come across one, be sure to explore the avenue. You may just be able to strike an opportunity that will go on to serve you for a lifetime.

Finally, if your business is struggling, you are doing something wrong. Revisit your business plan and try to find out what is not working. Once again, if this is not your forte, consider getting some help by either hiring an expert or consulting someone who knows how business plans work.

With that said, all that remains now is for you to put all of this into action and go on to explore your own success. You have learned everything that I could have offered. From one candle maker to another candle maker, I bid you farewell, and I wish you the best of luck.

Conclusion

Business of any kind requires commitment, knowledge, and patience. Candle making is no different. While there are hundreds of thousands of ideas out there, candle making is quite different and unique, and something that is easily overlooked by the masses. If you are someone who loves to create candles, and you have gone through this book successfully, congratulations! You are fully prepared to go on out there and create a business entity that will go on to serve you for a lifetime.

Yes, there are challenges, but that is what makes the entire journey so much more meaningful. I have ensured that I provided you with everything you need to get started, and that means that most of the issues you might face are already known to you. Using the knowledge that you have gained, this business, or any other for that matter, can get off the ground smoothly.

I promised you that I would teach you all about the candle making business, and would take you into the technicalities. To remind ourselves of what we learned, here is a quick look at some vital topics covered in this book:

- The candle making processes
- Types of candles we can create
- How and where to get your supplies from
- How to maintain quality
- How to jump-start your business
- Effective marketing and business planning
- Maintaining the momentum

We learned many things, but all of it will be in vain

should you decide to set this book aside and never go on to put the knowledge into action. Any business idea, at first, seems intimidating. It is only the first step that is scary. Once you take your first step, any journey, regardless of how long it may be, starts growing shorter pace by pace. Just keep the momentum going, and soon you should be realizing your dreams and your profits, and will be selling your candles like hot cakes.

I would love to know how this book was able to help you out, and whether this book provided you with some helpful knowledge. I know that I cannot gain your valuable feedback directly, which is why I will certainly keep an eye on the reviews section. If you found this book helpful and if you were able to learn something new and good, let me know. It is through your reviews that I gain the confidence to do more for the world.

Finally, it is time for us to part ways. I wish you a splendid journey ahead. I wish you the best of luck, and I hope that one day, I will be burning one of your candles at my next special occasion.

References

Bar Code Graphics Inc. (n.d.). *How to obtain a UPC.* GS1 UPC Barcodes. Retrieved August 21, 2020, from https://www.gs1-us.info/

Candle Science. (n.d.-a). *How to price your candles.* CandleScience - Candle and Soap Making Supplies. https://www.candlescience.com/how-to-price-your-candles

Candle Science. (n.d.-b). *Starting Your Own Candle Making Business: A Blueprint for Success.* CandleScience - Candle and Soap Making Supplies. https://www.candlescience.com/starting-your-own-candle-business-a-blueprint-for-success

Fisher, D. (2019, December 5). *How to Choose the Best Wax to Make Candles.* The Spruce Crafts. https://www.thesprucecrafts.com/waxes-for-candle-making-516770

Katsis, F. (2016, April 25). *Setting Up Your Candle Making Workspace.* Soycandles.Melbourne. https://soycandles.melbourne/2016/04/25/setting-up-your-candle-making-workspace/

National Candle Association. (n.d.). *Types of Candle Wicks | NCA.* National Candle Association. https://candles.org/elements-of-a-candle/wicks/

Walker, S. (n.d.). Candle Making Niche Report. In *nichehacks.com.* Retrieved August 19, 2020, from https://nichehacks.s3-us-west-2.amazonaws.com/assets/uploads/2014/09/Candle-Making-Advanced-Report.pdf

Made in the USA
Las Vegas, NV
14 December 2020

13293550R00075